BLOODY
ADJECTIVES

For Ruben who one day may ask:
"What did Grandad do?"

BLOODY ADJECTIVES

Ripping Yarns from Sleepy Hollow

PETER RHODES
of the Express & Star

BREWIN BOOKS

BREWIN BOOKS
19 Enfield Ind. Estate,
Redditch,
Worcestershire,
B97 6BY
www.brewinbooks.com

Published by Brewin Books 2021

A CIP catalogue record for this book is
available from the British Library.

ISBN: 978-1-85858-730-1

Printed and bound in Great Britain
by Severn

"The terminal at Sarajevo was the saddest place I had ever seen. Windows were shattered by gunfire and the floor, crunching beneath our feet, was carpeted in shards of broken glass and thousands of Kalashnikov cartridge cases. The place had been shot up, wrecked with gunfire by people with too many bullets and not enough brains. Yet on the counters, still open, were the booking forms, ticket stubs and boarding cards of a saner age. Here, frozen in time, was the moment when normality was overwhelmed by madness and the airport workers, without even closing their books, fled before the gunmen. A Mary Celeste of airports."

Acknowledgements

Journalists are great company. It has been my privilege over more than half a century to meet a vast number of them. We have shared happy and sad times, covered some huge stories, swapped some amazing anecdotes and learned from each other. Some were friends, others just travelling companions. Too many of them have died too soon. My thanks to the following:

Jack Algar, Jim Pritchard, Robin Clarke, Barry Salmon, Bruce Harrison, Charlie Porter, Nigel Jenkins, Nigel Robinson, Geoff Mayor, Dave Print, Yvonne McGregor, Richard Yates, Roger Draper, Alan Poole, Steve Howe, Mark Steeds, Nikki Lennox, Nick Harries, Brian King, John Phillpott, Geoffrey Elliott, Keith Whetstone, Sally Brompton, Tom Swain, Brian Walkeden, Janet Buckton, Mick Davis, Mitch Mitchinson, Chapman Pincher, Alan Clegg, Martin Bell, Douglas Grosvenor, Mike Woods, Derek Smith, Clem Lewis, Peter Henshall, Jonathan Daumler-Ford, Vicky McKee, Peter Ricketts, Keith Parker, Tom Quirke, Marion Brennan, Derek Tucker, James Windle, Roy Coates, Barry Cox, David Hotchkiss, Gerry Anderson, John Ogden, Adrian Faber, Keith Harrison, Andy Sibcy, John Boileau, Sandra Parsons, Eluned Bowen, Deanna Delamotta, Anne-Laure Domenichini, Victoria Tagg, Fred Bromwich, Tony Dickens, David Shukman, Ian Cobain, Julia Lawrence, Roy Williams, Tim Walters, Mark Green, Fran Cartwright, Roger Goodwin, Martin Cleaver, Michael Nicholson, Geoff Wright, Steve Derry, Tony Lennox,

Dave Bagnall, Mark Drew, Gavin Dickson. And many, many more.

In addition, special thanks to my wife Sally and my brother Tim for proof-reading, to Express & Star Editor Martin Wright for his enthusiastic support and to Garry Copeland, not only for his advice on this little book but for being the best features editor and colleague any writer could hope for.

Foreword

In his preface to *Three Men in a Boat* in 1889, Jerome K Jerome insisted his book was perfectly truthful: *"Its pages form the record of events that really happened. All that has been done is to colour them; and, for this, no extra charge has been made."*

The same applies to this little book. It is all done from memory and, in a perfect world, each chapter would begin with "As I think I remember…" or "I seem to recall…" but that would get tiresome.

Some names have been omitted or changed but the incidents are as I recall them, with occasional colour added. Would I swear on a Bible that they all happened exactly as I remember? Well, after 50 years, who could?

This book is a product of the Covid-19 pandemic when we older folk thought we would all be dead in a fortnight, and what had happened to that glittering autobiography we always intended to write?

So here it is, a sackful of random memories rattled out in a few weeks of frantic typing during lockdown. It began as something for my family and for readers of the Express & Star, who have put up with me since 1985, but grew into something that may ring a bell, and perhaps raise a smile with journalists and readers everywhere.

All journalists like to think they saw the golden age of journalism but those of us who were in the trade from the 1960s to the 1990s experienced something special. It was an age when the great regional daily newspapers were making huge profits, reaching millions of readers and wielding great political power – especially those circulating in marginal parliamentary constituencies.

We writers, whether reporting to Newsdesk, Sports Desk or the so-called "Sleepy Hollow" that is Features, travelled the world in search of scoops, competing with Fleet Street and meeting princes, paupers, pools winners and celebrities.

I was lucky on two counts. Firstly, to survive in the troubled world of journalism for more than fifty years. Secondly, to avoid any job title involving the word "editor" and sticking to the old craft of writing. If you write enough, for long enough and are lucky enough, some of your yarns will be ripping yarns.

They were glory days, producing some glorious tales and I'm delighted to share some of them with you. Extracts from the Express & Star appear by kind permission of the Midland News Association.

Peter Rhodes
March 2021

Early Days

"There's so much violence today," the aged court usher complained during a recess in one particularly unpleasant assault case at Leamington Spa magistrates' court in 1970. "When I was a lad there was nothing like this, no violence." He thought for a moment, wistfully, and continued: "Mind you, if a new kid came to the village we'd all tie him to the church gate and piss all over him. But there was no violence…"

I entered journalism in July 1969, a few days after the Americans landed on the moon. The Editor was an old friend of the family and I'd been interviewed by him some months before for a vacancy as trainee reporter. Today, journalism is a career for graduates; back then, A-levels at 18 or even a good clutch of O-levels for a smart 16-year-old were enough to get a promising school-leaver on the three-year apprenticeship designed by the NCTJ, the National Council for the Training of Journalists.

"If you get two A-levels you can have the job," said the Editor. He went on to explain that the pay was £9 15 shillings (£9.75) a week.

"I know it doesn't seem a lot," he smiled painfully, "but it is the union rate." I was young and naïve and formed the impression that the Editor would dearly love to pay more, much more, but alas his hands were tied by the wicked unions. I was some months in the job before I discovered that wasn't quite how collective bargaining worked.

A few weeks later I passed three A-levels without great distinction and, on a bright Monday morning in Leamington Spa, entered a room bearing a name that thrilled me then and still thrills me now: "Editorial," announced the small enamelled plate on the door.

If you have any imagination (and there's no point entering this business if you haven't), there is hardly an operating name in newspapers that doesn't stir the soul: Editorial, Newsdesk, City Desk, Foreign Desk, Sports Desk all resonate with dreams of exciting assignments in fabulous places. Sometimes, the title does not live up to expectations. Once, sent to cover a non-league football match at Tadcaster, I was told by the chief reporter to use the Press Box. Oh, the glamour. I imagined a glass-fronted eyrie packed with top-flight sports reporters breathlessly dictating their copy into a dazzling array of telephones and radio sets. It turned out that the Press Box at Tadcaster was something you stood on.

"For a better view," the chief reporter added helpfully. It was an old beer crate.

The first few weeks with Heart of England Newspapers in 1969 was an introduction to the engine rooms of society, the things that hold the system together and which most folk barely get involved in: council meetings, magistrates' courts, inquests. Stories were directed as appropriate to the groups' weekly newspapers: Leamington Spa Courier, Warwick Advertiser, Kenilworth Weekly News and also to the Leamington Morning News, a daily tabloid of just four pages which sold for 3d and was generally recognised as the smallest daily newspaper in Britain. For all its modest size, the Morning News gave trainee reporters an invaluable leg-up – daily newspaper experience. There is a world of difference between writing for a weekly newspaper and a daily where deadlines are tight and every day, no matter how quiet, must produce a good, strong, local front-page lead story.

Shortly before I joined there had been a heated debate in the town council over the future of the site of a demolished church. Most councillors favoured a multi-storey car park. Only the First Citizen of the Borough came out against it and in favour of a formal garden. The Morning News duly carried the headline: "Mayor Fights Erection in Town Centre." I have to add that though I searched through the Morning News archives, I never found this headline.

In truth, some much-loved newspaper yarns do not stand up well to fact-checking. So you probably won't find the classic report of a man who with his bare hands killed a pitbull terrier as it attacked a toddler in a Scottish town. For its first edition the local newspaper carried the headline: "Hero saves toddler from devil dog." It then emerged that the hero was a tourist from Wolverhampton. For later editions the headline was: "Englishman kills family pet."

However, while you may seek in vain for classic missprints and double-entendre headlines, some are most certainly genuine and languishing in the archives, including the rather gushy piece by a young reporter about being given a guided tour of a stately home by its aristocratic former occupant. She described: "The Great Hall at Weston Park where Lord Bradford holds his balls and dances."

Nor is there any doubt about this little gem which I spotted many years ago in the rather staid property columns of the upmarket Birmingham Post: "Unexpectedly back on the market – Twatling House." You may find nothing unexpected about a house with such a name failing to find a buyer, especially when you read on to discover the full address is Twatling House, Lickey End.

Also 100 per cent genuine is this, from the Club Notes section of the Express & Star many years ago, describing a mystery trip: "During the trip, a competition was held to see if anyone could guess where the coach was going. The prize, a bottle of whisky, was won by the driver who correctly stated the tour would be held in the Clee Hill area." And, also from the E&S, this gripping 1960s drama review concerning an actor who doesn't quite grasp the part: "Although he tried his best to settle into the character, his stiffness returned whenever he was faced with a romantic scene."

Meanwhile, back in 1969, one of my earliest jobs on the Courier was to interview the owner of what used to be called a poodle parlour who had branched out from the usual clip and curl into dyeing little dogs their owners' favourite colour. I asked the questions and the photographer did his stuff, snapping away busily at two well-behaved little poodles. There was an issue looming in this interview. I was born colour-blind. It was my red-green deficiency, I used to tell people, that prevented my following my dream career and becoming a test pilot in the RAF. To tell the truth, there were other factors such as an inability to grasp the basics of physics, three failed attempts at Maths O-level and general academic incompetence and idleness. But here, as a working journalist, the colour-blind question could not be dodged.

"So do you have any dogs you've actually dyed?" I asked the manager.

"How do you mean?"

"You know. Dogs that you've dyed an unusual colour."

"These are them," she replied, pointing at the two poodles in some irritation, as though I was dismissing her dog-dyeing skills.

4

"Really? So what colours are they?"

"This one," she explained acidly as if dealing with a particularly perverse moron, "is shocking pink. And this one is ice blue."

And that's what I told the Courier readers even if I couldn't see it myself. The thing about being colour blind is you relate colours to objects. Thus, grass is green, apples are red and oranges are orange. And poodles are poodle-coloured. It is hard to explain to people with perfect colour perception who usually ask: "How do you manage at traffic lights?" The answer is that the authorities thoughtfully put the stop light at the top, the go light at the bottom and the other one in the middle. And we colour-blind folk are happy to describe them as red, amber and green even though we know they are actually orange, yellow and grey.

For a grammar-school boy from a settled, comfortable home, the local magistrates' courts, with their daily diet of sex, violence and congenital stupidity, were a mystery. Where did all these thick people come from? Why did they keep getting into trouble? And why did half-a-dozen local families seem to occupy half the charge-sheets?

Defendants were kept in line by Henry, an aged and permanently angry court usher who demanded respect for what he regarded as his court.

"I swear by Almighty God…" began one defendant in the dock.

"Get yer 'ands out of yer pockets!" interjected Henry before allowing the sacred oath to continue.

The magistrates' court system in the 1970s was much as it had been for the previous 100 years with justice dispensed by the upper, white and professional classes on the lower, manual and increasing black, orders. Before the wholesale reforms of PACE – the 1984 Police and Criminal Evidence Act – some of the prosecutions were at best questionable. I recall two troubling conversations, the first with a police sergeant whose job was to outline the prosecution to the bench of, usually, three magistrates. "I've always taken the view," he said cheerfully, "that if we weren't sure we had enough evidence, you could rely on the magistrates to sort it out." Which would have been fine, were it not for the other conversation at about the same time, with a magistrate who confided: "I've always taken the view that if they hadn't done something wrong, the police wouldn't have arrested them in the first place." It was not a recipe for the closest possible examination of the evidence, assuming there was much evidence.

Magistrates were literally a law unto themselves. I remember one theft case where, on the flimsiest of evidence and to the astonishment of the defending solicitor, the bench delivered a verdict of guilty on a defendant who had no previous convictions but a troubled home life. Some days later I was chatting to the chairman of that bench and couldn't help observing that this conviction seemed unfair. "Look," the JP explained pragmatically. "He needed help. We convicted him which means he'll get help from a probation officer. If we'd acquitted him, he'd get nothing." There was a certain logic about it but what sort of system could reach out to a vulnerable person only by giving him a criminal record?

Another court, another case. Some years later, working on the Evening Mail in Birmingham, I applied for a job on the Express & Star at Wolverhampton.

"You'll need subtitles up there," growled an old Brummie hack.

"Why's that?"

"Different language," he explained wearily, having just finished a trying day at the city's Crown Court. Much of the opening session had been spent agreeing a common tongue. Courts prefer simple, straightforward yes and no answers. This defendant, like so many Black Country folk, rarely used the word "yes."

"You are James Willie Boggins?" the clerk to the court asked the defendant.

"Ar."

"I'm sorry, what was that?"

"I said ar. I'm James Willie Boggins."

"Mr Boggins. This is a court of law. May I ask you to answer questions with a yes or no."

"Ar," beamed the defendant.

"No, that won't do. When you say 'ar' presumably you mean 'yes'?"

"Ar."

Then may I ask you in future to use the word 'yes'?"

"Ar."

After some coaching, the defendant began answering 'ar, yes' which was close enough for the judge and the trial proceeded, only to run into the treacherous twin rapids of a Black Country accent coupled with a barrister who had not read his briefs too closely. It was an assault case and the accused's alibi was that on the day in question he had been visiting Symonds Yat, the beauty spot on the River Wye.

"So, Mr Boggins," began his barrister. "Where do you say you were on the date of the alleged offence?"

"Sir," replied Boggins, "I wor at Symonds Yat."

"Where was he?" interjected the judge.

"I wor at Symonds Yat," the accused repeated, helpfully.

7

"No wiser," said the judge.

The barrister shuffled frantically through his papers. "M'Lud," he said in an inspired moment. "I believe Mr Boggins is saying he was on someone's yacht."

But that was for the future. Back in the flower-power summer of 1969, I was loving the job. The other half-dozen reporters were a little older than me and I admired everything about them from the cool, unaffected way they smoked to how they held the phone in the crook of their neck while dictating copy from the pub nearest the court, simultaneously demolishing a pint and a cheese cob as the juke box endlessly played the hit of the day, Glen Campbell's Wichita Lineman.

Filing copy in close proximity to the court was always a risky affair, as defendants drank cheek-by-biro with reporters. I recall phoning one item and delivering the closing line: "The judge said McGregor was a persistent drunk, womaniser and wife beater who richly merited a custodial sentence" just as McGregor himself, released on a suspended sentence, stalked into the pub and scowled at me. A larger reporter inserted himself protectively between me and the aggrieved subject of my report. They were a good bunch of colleagues, even the elderly chief sub who once berated me for my appalling lack of knowledge about the 1879 Zulu War.

Time after time in this craft of ours, old rubs up against young. Many of the grown-ups sharing their newsrooms with us kids in the 1970s had been fighting in the Second World War less than 30 years before. They had witnessed the most appalling sights, lost their best friends, seen their cities blitzed and then found themselves in a world where supercilious young men with far too much hair knew nothing about the war, cared less and believed that All You Need is Love. In my teens I wore a button badge proclaiming: "Wars will cease when men refuse to fight" and could not understand why the deputy headmaster, a gunner veteran of Italy and Normandy, found it offensive.

The editor of the Warwick Advertiser in the 1960-70s was Jim Pritchard, a mustardy old infantry officer who had fought in Burma and would not allow any of us reporters to use the term "torrential rain" on the grounds that if you've never seen the monsoon, you've no idea. He ran a tight ship. My weekly expenses form was once rejected by him with the admonition to "stop playing the big boy and flashing your money about." This, for a 25p bar bill.

On one occasion he asked the theatre critic to do an extra night job and the critic objected. "Richard Yates!" stormed Jim Pritchard. "I've sent better men than you out to their deaths." Naturally, the phrase passed into the office's folklore and became a popular greeting between us hacks. Years later at a Heart of England reunion, I had a drink with Jim Pritchard as we waited for the rest of the old timers, including Richard Yates, to arrive. The old editor was nervous. "You know," he confided, "I once told Yates that I'd sent better men than him out to their deaths. Do you think anyone remembers?" For a moment I had a flashback to the tale of the Earl of Oxford, as related in John Aubrey's Brief Lives. The Earl had bowed deeply to Elizabeth I and farted loudly. Overcome with shame he fled the court and spent seven years away. On his return the Queen greeted him with: "My Lord, I had forgot the fart." Good Queen Bess forgot the fart and we hacks had entirely forgotten Jim Pritchard sending better men than Richard Yates to their death. I assured Mr Pritchard that none of us could recall any such incident.

Every newspaper I have worked on has had a running feud between the old 'uns who know exactly how to produce newspapers and the young 'uns who are desperate to break the mould and try something new. No anecdote better illustrates this than a piece by the peerless sports writer Frank Keating who in 1993 paid tribute to the old-style sporting supplements, usually referred to as "pinks." His yarn involves a fresh young sports editor trying to get a grizzled old freelance sports reporter at Barnsley to inject some descriptive colour into his match reports and, above all, to drop his routinely permanent opening line: "The Reds kicked off with a rush." In fact, the new sports editor felt so strongly about this that he threatened the stringer with the sack if any more match reports began with: "The Reds kicked off with a rush." At the next match, seethingly obeying orders, this is what the old chap wrote: *"Oakwell glistened after the rains and a sharply textured and almost translucent winter's sunlight, reminiscent of Bruegel's vivid brushwork, helped warm the easterly zephyrs which lanced across the ground. And while it bent low the scurrying, Lowry-type latecomers to the match, it stirred into picturesque wisps the smoke from the surrounding chimneys as the white-kneed official in black shrilly set things in motion with a sharp whistle-blast – and the Reds kicked off with a rush."*

Glorious stuff.

Fatal...

In my first few weeks at Leamington the job was a lark, a spree, a hoot with a brown paper envelope containing £9 15 shillings, minus tax, at the end of it. And then one sunny day in the autumn of '69, things changed. I was sent with a photographer to a house fire. As we walked up the lane, a fire officer was coming the other way.

"Much in it?" asked the photographer.

"Fatal," said the officer.

Fatal? Someone was dead? I was shocked to be at the scene of a stranger's death, shocked an hour or so later to be turning one family's tragedy into front-page news. That was the moment the job turned serious and for a fleeting moment I felt: "I never signed up for this." Later in the day the chief reporter read my copy, made a couple of changes and said: "Remember, Peter, just because you wake up fit and healthy in the morning it's no guarantee that you'll still be alive by bedtime." He was right. Time after time, the sheer randomness of sudden death shocks and bewilders us hacks. The child who falls from her bicycle on the riverside path and drowns. The farmer who catches his sleeve in a tractor power shaft and bleeds to death. The folk settling down to an evening by the telly in a little town called Lockerbie. They all got out of bed that morning.

Strangely enough, 20-odd years later, I interviewed a man who had written a book on the subject of spontaneous combustion of human beings. I described my first fatal fire to him and he reckoned it fitted the bill. However, like so many other spontaneous-combustion claims, it involved an old and infirm person sitting in front of a fire. I have no doubt that the human body can be reduced to ash in a fire. Whether that fire can erupt independently within something as watery as the human body is another matter.

After a few weeks, I was entrusted with what later generations of journalists would call the death knock, although we would never have used that term. For a start, it's disrespectful. Secondly, it over-dramatises what was usually a positive encounter. Every few weeks somebody on our patch would be killed on the roads. The job of the local reporter was to call on the family, do the interview, obtain a photo of the deceased if possible and produce an obituary for the next edition, often including an appeal for witnesses from the police. It was a regular Monday-morning task after the weekend crop of accidents. Sadly, the victims were often teenagers, some only sixteen, killed on motorbikes or mopeds. I must have done dozens of these sad, untimely interviews. Once I was chased off the doorstep by a protective neighbour and once, a few minutes into the interview, the mother of the dead girl changed her mind, asked for my notebook and tore out the pages. But as a rule people understood we had a job to do and they wanted something in the paper to acknowledge their loss and pay tribute to a life cut short. Sometimes, the family didn't want to talk and the only decent option was to walk away. But some reporters, having been promoted to news editors, seemed to have been stripped of much decency. They took the view that if someone didn't want to speak to the paper, they were the enemy. And it was your job to knock on the neighbours' doors until someone came up with the goods. This explains how I came to report from a number of strangely deserted streets.

"You mean none of these neighbours were in?" snarled the news editor suspiciously.

"That's right," I lied. "None of them."

"So what about the local shops?"

"There aren't any," I lied again, having just bought twenty Rothmans at the Spar.

The interview and obituary that caused the most heartache, and still haunts me fifty-odd years later, involved a message from newsdesk about a young motorcyclist killed in a crash after leaving a local pub at 10pm. Police wanted witnesses.

I knocked at the family's door. The father welcomed me in. He spoke proudly and lovingly of his lad. He produced a number of photos for us to use. I told him about the police appeal.

"That's good," he said. "But he didn't leave the pub at 10pm. It was 8pm. He hadn't been drinking all night or anything like that."

Back at the office I re-checked the time.

"Yeah, it was 10pm," said the news editor impatiently. "Now, get that story written."

And so I did, giving the time as 10pm because, whatever the father thought, that was the time given to us by the police. Soon after the first edition appeared, the father rang me, furious and tearful.

"How could you print such a pack of lies?" he demanded. "I told you it was 8pm, not 10pm."

Again I rang the news editor. Was he absolutely sure about the time?

"Bloody hell, yes. I've got the police report in front of me. It says he left the pub at 2000 hours and that's 10pm, isn't it?" And then he laughed (I particularly remember the laugh) and added: "Sorry, no. It's 8pm, isn't it?"

I can't apologise for someone else's mistake but from that day to this I have always been very wary of the 24-hour clock.

Since social media took over so many lives, the knocking at doors of the bereaved has become rarer. These days, local newspapers are more likely to rely on the tributes paid to the deceased on Facebook or Twitter. Inevitably, being posted by friends and family, these descriptions tend to be glowing and go unchallenged. For example, after a "devoted" father of five children dies in a gang fight in a city centre, no-one asks how the deceased squared his devotion to wife and kids with being in a night club until 4am. Here is a cynic's guide to online tributes. "He was the life and soul of the party" = alcoholic. "He stood up for his friends" = started fights. "Sensitive" = psychopath. "Gentle giant" = morbidly obese. "He will be missed by many" = he owed money all over town. "He did not suffer fools gladly" = workplace bully. And so on.

Plenty of give and take, dearie

As soon as I started at Heart of England I was given two regular jobs. The first was as Uncle Tom, editor of the weekly Young Courier Club, aimed at young readers. Uncle Tom's column began each week with "Hello, Boys and Girls!" followed by about 500 words of inspired general knowledge for kiddies or, more commonly, whatever the hack could dream up in a spare half-hour.

The great joy about a new trainee reporter joining the staff was that the incumbent Uncle Tom could dump the job, the title and all the brain-racking that went with it, on to the junior. I decided to write a weekly series about keeping pets. This was not a good idea. The weeks came round awfully quickly and the supply of suitable animals (dog, cat, hamster, mice etc) ran out after a couple of months. I considered branching out into horses and ponies but the Editor said this would inspire envy among the less well-off. He was wary, too, of tarantulas or anything else likely to bite Young Courier Club members.

In some despair, I hunted for inspiration in the Leamington Courier library – a small room lined with shelves and overseen by a pipe-smoking old gentleman called Romney who spent his days scissoring the latest Courier into separate stories and stashing them away for posterity. The combination of scissors, newspaper cuttings and a pipe was a permanent fire hazard and it was not unusual to see Romney dashing through the newsroom brandishing a blazing waste-paper bin and dumping it on the lawn outside. There was nothing scientific about Romney's filing system. Stories about people were filed under their names. Everything else went into a massive archive, which stretched around two sides of the room, called History of Leamington. Romney knew where every story was but none of us reporters had a clue.

The library also had a small collection of street directories and books of local history. Among these I found a pre-war travel guide to Warwickshire. Here, in one old volume, was the answer to Uncle Tom's prayers, a vast supply of Warwickshire villages if not from A to Z then at least from A to W. The next "Hello, Boys and Girls!" was followed by a shamelessly filched description of the delightful town of Alcester and in the weeks that followed Uncle Tom introduced his youthful followers to Bidford, Charlecote, Dunchurch, Exhall and so on. It ran alphabetically for some months and when the series ended, with a fine commentary on Wroxall, I had served my time and gleefully handed over the column to an even younger and fresher trainee reporter.

"Any ideas?" he asked me, glumly.

"You could always try tarantulas."

In the internet age, still 30 years in the future, my Warwickshire villages column would have been instantly Googled and exposed as plagiarism. But in the days of typewriters and reference books, I got away with it, although there were a couple of hairy moments, both involving vicars.

The first wrote in a tone of deep and quite un-Christian scepticism about Uncle Tom's description of his parish church which included a reference to an ancient Latin inscription on the church floor. The vicar pointed out that, by general agreement, the carving had been illegible for at least 100 years and, in any case, had been covered by a carpet since the 1950s.

The other vicar, bless him, was simply full of praise for my magnificent work in visiting and describing so many villages. He suggested I should compile all these weekly columns into a guide book. I felt this would be pushing my luck, and declined.

My other regular job on the Courier in 1969 was golden weddings. There were at least one or two a week and I quickly became an old hand at interviewing couples who had been married for 50 years. I prided myself on being able to put the answer to the key question in my notebook ("Plenty of give and take, dearie") before actually asking the question ("So what is the secret of a long and happy marriage?") Not that all those golden weddings were entirely happy. It was some time before I figured out why there were so many golden weddings in 1969. Do the maths. Fifty years earlier the lads had come home from the First World War and married their sweethearts or, in some cases, somebody else's sweetheart. About 700,000 young Britons were killed in what they called the Great War. For some heartbroken girls the choice was between becoming an old maid or accepting virtually any offer of marriage. Some of those couples discovered happiness over the years but some did not. There was not always great affection displayed in the golden-wedding photos in the Leamington Spa Courier. I recall one lady who, a few months after we featured her 50-year story, rang me with a simple message: "The old bugger's just died. I thought you might want to know." She was not exactly heartbroken.

I have always regretted not asking more questions of that generation of men. When I entered journalism, the lads of 1914-18 were all around us. They had seen and done the most extraordinary things. But they didn't talk and we didn't ask. They didn't talk because they were a generation raised to know its place and never to make a fuss. We didn't ask because, hey, this was the Swinging Sixties and who, in the groovy new age of flower power and love, wants to hear about whizzbangs over Ypres?

But in the years that followed, this silent generation found its voice and we Children of the Sixties became fascinated by their war and by what they had to say.

"We can get you buggers for a shilling a day"

In the early 1980s, working on the Coventry Evening Telegraph, I was looking for a background feature to go with the latest news about yet another crisis in the British motorcycle industry, this time at Triumph.

"You ought to speak to Sidney Sidwell," said the features editor. "He worked at Triumph for 50 years."

Sidney was small, cheerful and 85 and eager to chat about his beloved Triumphs in the glory days of British bikes. We talked for about an hour and as I got up to leave, I noticed a pair of highly polished brass shell cases on his fireplace.

"What's this all about?" I asked.

"I'll put the kettle on," said Sidney Sidwell. And he talked, and talked. Gunner Sidwell had been a part-time soldier, a

Territorial in the Warwickshire Royal Horse Artillery when war broke out in August 1914. He recalled the thrill of mobilisation, of gathering at the drill hall and entraining for London where their old 13-pounder guns were exchanged for 15-pounders. And then over to France where his unit earned its spurs as the first Territorial Force battery to open fire against the Germans. That's where the shell cases came from. As he told his tale he held one of the cases and exuded pure pride.

"Sugar?" he asked.

"No, thanks."

"You ought to have plenty of sugar," said Sidney, shovelling three teaspoons into his mug. "Sugar's good for you."

For a moment I thought of warning him of the dangers of sugar, from obesity to diabetes. But when you're talking to someone who opened fire on the Kaiser's hordes and has survived to 85, it's best to know your place.

Later, first on the Birmingham Evening Mail and then with the Express & Star, I helped arrange tours for some of the last survivors of the First World War to the battlefields of France and Flanders. It was high time we got their memories down. I organised a couple of battlefield pilgrimages with Tony and Valmai Holt who had recently founded Major & Mrs Holt's Battlefield Tours. Tony Holt gave me the simplest and most useful tip for visiting the immaculate war cemeteries in France and Flanders, "Don't just look at the white headstones. Try to imagine each of those stones as a young soldier in khaki."

A handful of Great War veterans, all in their 80s, accompanied each trip. Fred Cowles recalled the fortunes of war, the razor-slim chances that dictate someone will die and someone a few inches away will have another 60 years of life: "My corporal, Dick Nuttall, was using the Lewis gun. He fired about twenty magazines then said, 'Here, Fred, you have a go at this'. I stepped forward and he stepped backward to exactly where I had been. Three minutes later we were both on the ground. He was dead and I was hit in the leg and elbow."

John Powell was taken for dead after being caught in a shell blast: "When I woke up I was in the morgue. There were all these chaps covered in blankets on stretchers resting on trestles in this whacking great tent. I pushed the blanket off my face and two stretcher bearers saw me. They nearly died of shock."

John Powell recalled: "I remember a sergeant-major saying to me, 'We can get you buggers for a shilling a day but the horses cost eighty quid each'."

After visiting the battlefields we attended the evening ceremony at the Menin Gate where Fred Cowles, as a veteran, was invited to deliver the lines: "They shall grow not old as we that are left grow old. Age shall not weary them nor the years condemn. At the going-down of the sun and in the morning. We shall remember them." His voice faded almost to a whisper as he ended, tears flowing down his old cheeks. He braced up and threw a smart salute to his mates who never came home.

On one of those pilgrimages we climbed out of the shallow remains of a trench in the company of a delightful, soft-spoken veteran who, on July 1st 1916, had been a private in the Royal Warwickshire Regiment. He remembered going over the top into a whirlwind of lead and being puzzled to see, in his peripheral vision to left and right, his colleagues kneeling down. Not kneeling, but dying. By the end of that terrible day nearly 20,000 British Tommies were dead and 40,000 wounded. This old soldier's platoon started the day sixty strong. The following day only eighteen answered the roll call.

Sam Cutts, 100 years old when we met and by then a frail old man in a nursing home, described death by cold steel when he was an armed and agile infantryman at Gallipoli in 1915:

"One Turk came at me with his bayonet but when he was about five yards off he either stumbled or fainted so I stuck my bayonet in him. You see, we'd been told to kill or be killed, show no mercy, take no prisoners."

Back on the home front in Wolverhampton, Len Turner described how it felt, aged just six, to be bombed by a Zeppelin: "I could clearly see two men in a basket container underneath. They were dropping things out over the side. Of course, we hadn't a clue what they were."

And most memorably of all, Jack Laiste, a seventeen-year-old Lancer in the autumn of 1914, who wrote, in shattering detail, of his squadron's ferocious charge against a force of German uhlans (heavy cavalry). It is horrifying not merely because of the appalling wounds suffered by the men on both sides but because Jack was haunted for the rest of his days by the effect the skirmish had on Queenie, his horse: *"I pulled Queenie up and dismounted. She was covered with blood and white lather and I was covered with it, too. Queenie had a lump torn out of her shoulder and I had a finger hanging loose. I looked into her brown eyes. I was afraid to stroke her ears, which I used to do. I looked at her and she seemed to say, 'My God, what have you done to me?' She was trembling like a leaf and so was I."*

And another war

It was the passing of the Great War generation that made us realise, almost too late, that we had to turn memories into hard print. And so began the process of journalists talking to warriors and harvesting their stories, before the blinds came down. The Second World War produced many more recollections of warfare than the First, for the simple reason that there were more survivors to recall everything from Dunkirk, 1940, to the Japanese surrender in 1945. From many hundreds of powerful and moving testimonies, I choose this one, from 2007. I thought of it instantly in 2019 when some pundit on the radio declared: "It has never been harder to be a young person than it is today." If you seriously believe that, read this:

Four days out and homeward bound from Canada, something strange appeared on the radar of the ageing destroyer HMS Winchelsea.

'The shadow was appearing and then disappearing,' recalls Bob Lilley. His home in Castlecroft, Wolverhampton, is a world away from the freezing North Atlantic and the daily terrors of wartime convoy duty.

'We thought it might be a sub on the surface. The Old Man ordered us to run it down.'

But as HMS Winchelsea, a veteran of the First World War, swung into action, the object came into view. Not a German U-boat but a ship's lifeboat with one small sail taking her, with infinite slowness, on a westward course. Leading seaman Lilley was ordered to take command of the destroyer's cutter. With a team of men he ploughed through the calm grey sea toward the lifeboat. The sight that greeted him still haunts him. In the lifeboat were ten British merchant seamen. They were dead and frozen stiff and the seagulls had taken their eyes. Their vessel, probably a freighter, had been attacked by U-boats some days before. These doomed sailors had been given no time to take to the boats.

'Two of them were wearing only vests. They had obviously come straight out of the engine room.'

Adrift in the Atlantic in December, hundreds of miles from the Canadian coast, the sailors could only raise their pitiful sail, huddle together for warmth and hope for a rescue that never came. They perished along with more than 29,000 others of the British Merchant Navy in the six-year struggle to keep Britain supplied with food and munitions for the fight against Nazism. Their vanished freighter was one of 2,246 merchant ships lost. Back then, with the ever-present threat of U-boats, there was no time to reflect on their heroism. Winchelsea's cutter turned to the destroyer with the lifeboat in tow. The ten frozen bodies were lifted gently aboard. Leading Seaman Lilley had joined the Royal Navy in 1938, the year the war started. He had seen too many bodies to be shocked. But the sadness stays with him.

'The next day we buried them at sea.'

Bob Lilley had a great collection of photographs of his ship and the shipmates he served with through the darkest days of the Battle of the Atlantic. Then his house was burgled and the intruders stole the lot.

'I am a very disillusioned man. I often wonder if it was all worthwhile.'

And try as he might, even after all these years, he cannot shake off the memory of that lifeboat with its crew of ten dead men. How could he when it happened on a day usually associated with joy? Bob Lilley was a veteran with three years' service when he was ordered to intercept the drifting lifeboat. Yet he was just a boy of nineteen, a teenager in arms doing his duty – on Christmas Day, 1942.

Features? You mean Sleepy Hollow

I finished my apprenticeship at Heart of England Newspapers in the summer of 1972 and began looking for a bigger, better-paying paper. My fiancee Sally was at the University of York and the city's newspaper, the Yorkshire Evening Press, was a fine old hot-metal paper with offices and printworks smack in the middle of the city, with its reception in Coney Street and the back of the building overlooking the River Ouse. I applied for a job on the off-chance and received a reply saying they had no vacancies but would keep my letter on file. A few weeks later they summoned me for an interview with Jack White, the Editor, and I was offered the job of a head-office reporter on £27 a week. The big perk, the news editor told me as he showed me around, was that my duty night would be Fridays which meant lots of free dinners with the various trade guilds and trusts which ran the city. I would, of course, require a dinner jacket.

"So will the firm pay for that or do I put the suit hire on expenses?" I asked innocently. The news editor looked stern.

"Mr White takes the view," he explained with the air of one who had explained it many times before to many recruits, "that the sort of young gentleman who works for the Evening Press would already possess a dinner jacket."

My first week's salary was £27. The cost of a new dinner jacket from Burtons was £27. Not a profitable start.

But York's Friday night dinners lived up to their promise. The Company of Merchant Adventurers scored for excellent speeches and erudite conversation but for sheer, belly-busting quantity and quality, the York Butchers' Gild was unbeatable. I have never seen so much meat consumed by so few people.

York was a wonderful place to work, a sort of miniature London with its river, bridges, smart terraces and endless gossip. I stayed only a few months but that was long enough to loop-the-loop as the RAF unveiled its new Bulldog trainer at a local airfield, and to see a man jailed for poaching "in pursuit of coneys" near Wetherby, which seemed very 18th century although I was the only person in court who seemed shocked.

Justice in the city magistrates' court could be delivered quickly. One drunk-driver was hauled up into the spike-trimmed Victorian dock looking like death, only a few hours after being nicked.

"And how do you plead?" demanded the clerk.

"Er… er…" A sharp-eyed cop spotted what was about to happen, grabbed the defendant by the collar and whisked him down the stairs as he erupted in a fountain of vomit and deep remorse.

"Guilty," came the faint, damp plea from below.

They were robust times. One case of assaulting a police officer began with the clerk asking why the defendants, two thick-set locals, were so heavily bandaged.

"In the course of the assault," explained the prosecuting sergeant, "the officer was obliged to draw his nightstick."

The officer in question was in court with a small plaster over one eye. The defendants looked as though they had gone nine rounds with a kangaroo. You couldn't but wonder what sort of weapon was a night stick.

I had a strange interview in York with an old chap whose claim to fame was that he had worked for 50 years at the same brass foundry in the city. His boss, a friend of the editor, thought he was a jolly fine chap and deserved something in the paper. I was sent along with a photographer. He talked quietly about his five decades in brass. Yes, he'd enjoyed it, by and large, although he regretted being in a reserved profession and staying behind while all his mates joined the army in the Last Lot. He fell silent. And then, quite suddenly and unexpectedly, he burst into tears.

"I've wasted my life, haven't I?" he sobbed. "Totally wasted it."

I comforted him as best I could but there was nothing to say. I went back to the office and wrote up the interview. The photographer brought across his prints. The big difference I found in moving from a small weekly newspaper to a big daily was not a dramatic improvement in the standard of writing but in photography. The Evening Press photographers (or snappers as they hate being called) took great pride in their work. This one had posed the brass worker close against a jug he had made and the reflected golden glow of the brass illuminated his face.

The next day I was walking through the centre of York when someone burst from the crowd and shook me by the hand. It was the brass worker.

"Thanks so much for the piece you did," he smiled. "And the picture. It made me look really good. And sorry about that nonsense before."

But life on the Evening Press was not what I had hoped for. After a couple of months in head office I was promoted to district reporter responsible for a patch extending from Tadcaster in the south to Wetherby in the north. There was a small pay rise but no district office, no colleagues, no banter, no gossip. I was expected to work out of pubs and cafes and was issued with a GPO credit card to make calls from telephone boxes. If you have ever conducted an interview with a bereaved mother while balancing a phone in your neck, a notebook in your hand, and with an irate lorry driver banging on the door to make his call, you will know what a bleak experience it is. One day I pulled into a layby, switched off the engine and asked myself out loud: "What the hell am I doing here?"

A little later I saw a job advertised in UK Press Gazette at the Coventry Evening Telegraph as a district-office reporter, based at Leamington. The Editor was Keith Whetstone. I had the advantage of knowing both the patch and the Evening

Telegraph reporters working there, one of whom was leaving, hence the vacancy.

"So how much do you want?" asked Whetstone.

"Two thousand a year," I suggested. I was on about £1,500 a year at York and the Telegraph was a bigger paper. Two thousand seemed fair but Whetstone looked mortally wounded. He explained that the company rate for district-office reporters was £1,750.

"Well, yes, but I know the patch and I've got a book full of contacts." Editors are always impressed by a reporter's list of contacts even if, on closer inspection, it's just a collection of local councillors, press officers and cops. Whetstone squirmed dramatically.

"Okay, two thousand," he conceded as though the money was being ripped in big, bloody shards from his back. I found out the next day that the reporter I was replacing had been on £2,500.

Keith Whetstone was a wonderful editor who died too soon. In retirement he bought a vineyard in France and took great pride in his vintages. Some years later we met at the Royal Shakespeare Theatre in Stratford-upon-Avon and he boasted that he was now producing a thousand bottles a year.

"And where do you sell them?" I asked.

"Sell them?" gasped Keith Whetstone. "Are you mad?"

Politics, red and blue in tooth and claw

From 1973 to 1981 I worked for the Coventry Evening Telegraph, first as a district reporter. It was not the most challenging occupation. Leamington is a fairly quiet, law-abiding sort of place. Council debates were civilised and urban deprivation existed but was never a big issue. We covered our share of murders. When politics got exciting, during election campaigns, Tom the chief reporter kept the political jobs for himself on the grounds that he was experienced. How the other reporter and I were expected to gain experience was never explained. During one campaign the Labour legend Renee Short came to town to address a Labour Party meeting at the Royal Pump Room.

"Bit dull but you can do it if you like," Tom told me. "Nothing ever happens at these sort of things."

Nothing happened for about the first 30 seconds of that meeting. Then, as Short warmed to her theme, she was suddenly interrupted by a man in the audience who stepped into the centre aisle, shouting and denouncing her.

"Do not listen to this woman," he shrieked. "This woman is a member of an unassimilated minority." There was a gasp of outrage. The anger in the room became almost tangible. And then another man, a local councillor red with rage, stormed down the hall and punched the heckler hard in the face – he went down like a sack of potatoes. So this is politics? It was entertaining, surprising and definitely newsworthy. But I had not the faintest idea what was happening or why. As the meeting resumed and the bloody-nosed heckler was chucked out, a colleague from the Birmingham Post explained all. Renee Short was Jewish, her heckler was a leader of some far-right and anti-semitic group. The councillor who thumped him was a lifelong socialist of the Spanish Civil War generation. This was real politics, red and blue in tooth and claw with loyalties you could trace back to hunger marches and the International Brigade. Thirty years of political reporting followed but it was never quite so exciting again.

It was while working in Coventry on a brief attachment from the Leamington CET office that I came across the single bravest act I ever reported. A light aircraft crashed on playing fields just outside the city. A couple of builders working on a house nearby saw the crash and ran to the scene. There is nothing unusual in that. When a human life is at stake, ordinary men and women have enormous reserves of courage. But when they got to the plane, the pilot was clearly dead, the fuel tank had ruptured and petrol was dripping from the wreckage. It was an explosion waiting to happen and no-one would have blamed those two builders for running to safety. But they stayed. For a couple of frantic minutes they struggled with the pilot's harness, freed the body and carried it out of the danger area. They did it, as they explained to the Evening Telegraph later, because they could not bear the thought of a family going through the ordeal of having to identify a charred body. If they had done it on the battlefield they would have won medals. As it was, they received nothing more than the profound thanks of the pilot's loved ones. It was a deed that moved me then and moves me now as I write about it once again. A deed not only of bravery but of compassion and pure decency.

One morning in Leamington we had a call from a reader in the village of Kineton complaining that yet another lorry had slid off the road on a notorious bend which the locals described as a skid pan. They had been campaigning for years for the council to re-surface it, using asphalt with better grip. The deadline loomed and, to save time, I rang the council for a response before going out to the scene.

"Ah, yes, Mr Rhodes," said the highways officials with a weary air. "We are fully aware of this." He went on to explain that, despite local concerns, this road met all the relevant highways standards for adhesion and had been tested and re-tested by engineers using state-of-the-art equipment. In short, he was telling us: Problem, what problem? Thus reassured, Brian the photographer and I drove down to Kineton to meet the locals. We parked on the bend in question. As he got out of the car Brian fell flat on his backside followed, a micro-second later, by me also falling on my backside. That road surface was like ice forming on grease. Never again have I taken the assurances of an official over the testimony of people on the spot.

News reporting is fine but tends to be repetitive. Some days it seems you are almost writing in templates from the day before: "A Leamington man today pleaded guilty," etc... "Police are hunting sticky-fingered raiders after a break-in at a toffee factory…" and so on.

And then there was an odd sort of Agatha Christie-type homicide on our patch. A man was accused of murdering his wife with arsenic. His alleged motive was to be free to marry his girlfriend. After the case, Pat Tracey, a local freelance working for one of the nationals, got an interview with the girlfriend and produced a long background piece. It contained the sentence: "Elaine tugged nervously at the top of her green leather boot as she gazed out impassively over the frozen Warwickshire countryside."

Wow. In that split-second I knew this was what I wanted to do. I'd done enough inquests, courts and council meetings. I wanted to be producing thousand-word pieces about glamorous women tugging their boots and gazing impassively.

"I want to work in Features," I told the chief reporter, Tom.

"Features?" he sneered. "You mean Sleepy Hollow?"

Journalists who think of themselves as 'ard-nosed 'acks often regard features as a sort of rest home for journalists who are getting past it. The reality is that feature writers, critics and columnists are the ones who give the newspaper its personality. They produce more column inches, usually better written and often to tighter deadlines, than news reporters. Because every feature carries their byline, they take a special responsibility for their work. All feature writers can do the news reporter's job but not every reporter will make a feature writer. And when times get hard and circulation falls, it is the papers with a special identity and a good crew of opinionated writers that hang on to their readers. The reporter writes his 200-word exclusive and has gone home long before the feature writer has completed the 1,000-word backgrounder on the story. Sleepy Hollow? If only.

But the argument was academic. There were only four or five feature writers on the Coventry Evening Telegraph and each of them was cherished by the Editor. They not only provided quality writing but were known faces, celebrities in the community. Readers wanted to know what Janet, Derek, David, Douglas or Muriel had to say. No mere reporter stood a chance of getting into Features unless somebody died.

And just then, somebody died.

One of the feature writers' maiden aunts passed away, leaving her a legacy. She never needed to write again and promptly put in her notice. I was summoned to Coventry, welcomed to Features and given a weekly column, On The Rhodes Side. I cleared my desk at Leamington while Tom quietly raged.

"You, you, you'll be off to Coventry and using them bloody…" he searched for the elusive word. "Them bloody adjectives."

In the new world of Features with its longer deadlines, longer articles and all them bloody adjectives, I was particularly glad to be away from one part of the news routine. As a reporter over the past 10 years I had covered dozens of inquests. The more I covered, the more I found them upsetting. Deaths must be investigated and the best coroners make the process as easy as possible for the bereaved. But there is no easy way of telling a wife that her husband committed suicide especially if he died, as sometimes happened, from pursuing the perfect orgasm by self-suffocation. There is no kind way of explaining to a father that his botched DIY wiring caused his child's electrocution.

Like any other court, inquests bring together people from all backgrounds. On one occasion in the 1970s, a car driver was killed when his vehicle ran off the road. The only eye witness was a lorry driver who came to the inquest straight from work, wearing his blue boiler suit. He described how the car driver was alive for some minutes after the accident and seemed to be trying to speak. This version was immediately challenged by the pathologist, a well-spoken professional in an expensive pale-grey suit. Having examined the organs of the deceased, he was sure this driver had suffered a massive heart attack. Death would have been instantaneous. So was it accidental death, as the lorry driver's account suggested, or was the driver dead at the wheel before the collision, in which case this was death by natural causes? The jury retired and came back with the natural-causes verdict, choosing the professional's opinion over the working man's eye-witness account. When people talk about society becoming less deferential, this is the incident I remember. I don't believe a modern inquest jury would dismiss the trucker's account so swiftly, or trust the professional so implicitly.

A few weeks later the Coroner announced that he had asked the High Court to quash the natural-causes verdict. A new inquest would be held. It turned out the pathologist had examined the wrong person's organs.

Three days on the lavvy

Newspapers love competitions, whether their own or other organisations. Joe Public suddenly winning a fortune out of the blue, whether it's a million quid on the Lotto or a smart new kitchen from the local newspaper, it usually makes a great, happy story. But not always. I recall interviewing one Lotto winner, a woman in her 70s who had scooped £4 million and was frightened to death of the consequences. God only knows why she hadn't asked Lotto for no publicity.

"Has this jackpot brought you any happiness yet?" I asked.

"No," she said wanly. "I've spent the last three days just sitting on the lavvy."

In 1971 we covered a huge football-pools win on our patch. The winner was a local man, Ron, and I was on copy-taking duty that afternoon, typing down the story as the reporter phoned it in. It was a win that would be dwarfed by later multi-million jackpots but at the time it seemed colossal and as I typed the sum, the numbers seemed to go on forever. It was enough to buy a new home, new cars and you could probably invest the rest and live handsomely on the interest. This win was a passport to a life of luxury.

Sadly, it didn't work out like that. A few years later we got word that Ron was hard-up and running a stall on the local market. He was one of the good guys, never bitter, probably too generous and always happy to talk to the press. I was dispatched to the millionaires' row to the south of Birmingham where we believed – wrongly, as it turned out – Ron and his family lived.

Let us pause this story here.

A few years after Ron's win we got a whisper that there had been an even bigger pools win on our patch. This time the win was about £500,000 and the winner's name was not revealed. But someone in the office had heard from someone at the pub that it was somebody (let us call him Charlie) who lived in a remote bungalow just outside the town. I was sent to the address with a photographer to see if we could persuade Charlie to lift his anonymity and give us the story.

Charlie roared with laughter. He thought the whole tale was hilarious. He'd heard it the night before and the only explanation he could offer was that the real winner had a similar surname to his. But it wasn't Charlie.

"If only," he grinned widely.

Never go back to the office empty-handed. Eager to get some sort of story, I tried another angle. Was he happy to be known as the bloke who, despite the rumours, hadn't won half-a-million? Charlie thought this was a great idea. It would explain the facts. It would take the pressure off him. So while I made my notes, the photographer took Charlie outside for a photograph indicating disappointment. Press photographers and picture editors like working with old, familiar and well-used poses. If someone wins a travel scholarship, the photograph shows them holding a globe and indicating their destination. If they have good news they give the camera a big thumbs-up. If the entire family is celebrating, they obligingly smile and stand in a line with their arms over each others' shoulders while kicking their right legs to the left. It pays to ensure the photographer, if working alone, is fully briefed about the nature of the story. Be aware, too, of the average press photographer's astonishing ability to coax his subjects into doing what he wants. I recall a picture editor opening with despair a selection of prints showing a smiling family doing the arms-on-shoulders and leg-kicking thing.

"I can't use these," sighed the picture editor.

"Why not?" I asked, "they're obviously a nice, happy family. Why else would they all be kicking their legs in the air?"

"Maybe so. But the story's about their dog being knocked down and killed."

Back at Charlie's house the photographer finished his work and Charlie was still laughing. We shook hands and parted.

"Better luck next time," I said.

"No chance," said Charlie. "I don't even do the pools."

We duly carried the story: "I'm Not the Mystery Pools Winner, says Charlie" (thumbs down) and thought no more about it.

Fast-forward a few years. The first pools winner, Ron, had gone bust and I was sent to interview him at his supposed home in millionaires' row. It was a splendid avenue reserved for the extremely rich. I didn't know which house, if any, was his and resorted to knocking on each door in turn. There was no answer at the first couple of houses. At the third the door opened and a fit, tanned and obviously well-to-do 60-something man answered. It wasn't Ron. It was Charlie.

Newspapers' own competitions are always popular, even if the winners aren't always exactly what you want. I was once dispatched from Coventry to a leafy, well-heeled avenue to tell a reader that she had won a fabulous £5,000 conservatory in an Evening Telegraph competition just for answering a couple of questions and thinking up a snappy sales slogan for Messrs Bloggs Paints & Rollers. Her house was a mansion and she and her husband had already spent tens of thousands of pounds re-creating it to suit their minimalist and hugely expensive tastes. For some readers, a new conservatory was a dream come true. For this pair it was a nice little extra, a little bon-bon of icing on a rich and enormous cake of well-sugared affluence. And no, she insisted, they really didn't want their photographs in the paper. In fact (cruellest barb of all) they weren't even Evening Telegraph readers. She had simply bought one copy on the strength of the competition advertised on the front page.

It is this sort of outcome, familiar to all newspaper features departments, that may explain, if not excuse, the following yarn in a city which will remain unnamed and at a time undivulged.

The prize was the biggest we had ever offered – a £20,000 luxury chalet on the mid-Wales coast. This may not strike you as particularly exotic but never assume that everybody – particularly working-class readers of a city newspaper, dream of far-flung baking-hot places with strange-sounding names. Our experience, time and again, was that a prize holiday of two weeks in Barbados might attract a few dozen entries but the offer of a week in a caravan at Barmouth would rupture entire teams of postmen as they dragged the mail sacks, bulging with competition entries, into the building. A chalet in mid-Wales was the perfect prize for our readers and, sure enough, we had thousands of entries. And because the quiz questions were dead easy, virtually all were 100 per cent correct and thus potential winners. We dumped them in a big black bin for the assistant editor to make the draw which he did by beating a dramatic drum-roll with his palms on the desk and then plunging his arm into the bin of entries. He pulled one out and read aloud:

"Mr J Gobbit, Flanders Avenue, Leighton Buzzard." There was a moment's silence.

"Well, bollocks to that," he continued seamlessly, chucking the winning entry in a waste-paper bin.

"What? You can't do that!" said the features editor.

"I bloody well can and I will," said the other. "Look, this is a city newspaper for city people who are our readers. This is the biggest prize we've ever had and I'm not giving it to someone from bloody Leighton Buzzard who probably bought a copy of the paper at the station and has never read it before or since. And in any case," he went on, pulling out another entry form from a local reader and declaring it the winner, "just see what it says in the small print."

Sure enough, the competition rules ended with: "In the event of a dispute, the Editor's decision is final." And so it was.

Two royal weddings and a funeral

Prince Charles and Lady Diana Spencer announced their engagement in February 1981 and preparations began for the greatest royal wedding of the age, to be held in St Paul's Cathedral on July 29. A series of briefings and dress rehearsals were arranged for the national and provincial press, a select number of whom – including me representing the Coventry Evening Telegraph – would be seated out of camera-shot in a cramped and tautological mini-grandstand in the

South Transept, just a few feet from the Queen and the Royal Family. Observing the ceremony was one thing. But how, in an age before mobile phones and digital cameras, would we get our copy and pix out of the cathedral and back home in time for our afternoon deadlines?

The solution, agreed between the media and the St Paul's authorities, was charmingly medieval. We writers were each issued with a small velvet bag with a drawstring neck – the sort of bag you might expect to find Maundy Money in – and a length of cord. The idea was that we would write our account of the wedding on notepaper, put the story in the velvet bag and lower it to the waiting clergy below who would hand it to another reporter who would then find a phone box and dictate our deathless prose to a copy typist at the newspaper's head office. As he handed out the little velvet bags, a clergyman briefed us hacks on the importance of not merely observing the ceremony but becoming involved in it. It was our duty, he explained piously, to sing the hymns. We smiled politely. Journalists simply love being told how to do their job.

It was a sweet plan but I couldn't see it working and I certainly didn't want to be experimenting with little bags and lengths of cord with a deadline approaching. I had time, all being well, to dash out of the Cathedral by the back door at the end of the service and run to the CET London office a few hundred yards away off Fleet Street, and use the phone there. But as a precaution I also filed what we call a holding piece, written and phoned at a leisurely pace from my hotel room near Green Park, the evening before the wedding.

In theory, the holding piece is disposable, used for one or two editions but then chucked away to make room for the main piece which is filed as close to deadline as possible with all the latest news. The reality, time after time, is that editors and sub-editors get twitchy as deadline approaches and stick with the holding piece, slotting the live story in whatever space is left.

And that's what happened on that glorious July day in '81. Before I even entered St Paul's I had filed a thousand-word backgrounder which back in Coventry they headlined: "Shared Day of Joy," based on interviews among the vast crowds lining the streets, with added anecdotes, a hefty dash of colour and some lines nicked from great literature. I am a believer in borrowing from the writings of the greats. It is a win-win option. If the reader doesn't recognise the quote, he assumes you've invented it, and what a brilliantly original turn of phrase it is. If he does recognise the quote, he feels a sense of kinship with the writer. See? We both know where that came from – aren't we erudite? This is how that piece ended:

"This joyous tide in the affairs of men sweeps excited folk along in their hundreds of thousands ... The wedding of a lifetime catches the eyes of the world and the goodwill here has to be seen to be believed. It is like Christmas going on forever. And those of us here, at the very heart of things, have a story for our children and grandchildren. For when Prince Charles pledged undying love to the blushing English rose of his heart, we were there – by golly, we were there!"

My live report from the cathedral was shorter and, being dictated against the clock after my heroic, sweaty run through the streets of London, was not as good as it might have been. Still, the subs put on the headline *"Dazzled, We All Blinked the Tears Away,"* cut it to fit and fitted it on the top of the page with my colour piece below. Job done.

Sadly, there was no room for a little vignette from the media grandstand in St Paul's where two American reporters behind me had some difficulty identifying the guests. Part of the problem is that easily recognised and important politicians are not so important at a royal wedding where the blood royal, no matter which royal house it is from, always outranks the people's democratic choices. An Arab prince in traditional gown and headgear entered and took his seat in the cathedral. "Who's that?" hissed one of the Americans. In a moment of mischief I told her it was Yasser Arafat, leader of the Palestinian Liberation Organisation and, at that time, one of the world's most wanted terrorists. She shared this information with a colleague. They discussed it in sharp whispers. There was a thoughtful pause. Then she leaned across to ask me: "So why is Yasser Arafat sitting in front of Nancy Reagan?"

I couldn't wait to get to a telly that evening and see the ceremony properly. From our much-envied press seats, we had only a thin sliver of visibility into the cathedral. I could hear Kiri Te Kanawa singing but all I could see of her was her feathered hat, bobbing and fluttering in the distance as though a parakeet had flown into St Paul's.

Ceremony over, report filed, I retraced my steps from Fleet Street to the cathedral in time to see the last ranks of the vast crowd vanishing down the hill towards Buckingham Palace, shimmering in the heat haze. The approaches to the cathedral were fouled with horse muck from the many carriages. The place stank. The uniforms, that wedding dress, the bands and guests in all their finery had departed leaving ordure behind. Years later, when Charles's "undying love" proved not so immortal, I was reminded of that scene as a metaphor for the fairy tale. Glamour, glitter, pomp and privilege on the top, horse shit underneath.

My second royal wedding was Prince Andrew's marriage to Sarah Ferguson at Westminster Abbey on July 23, 1986.

While every detail of the Charles / Diana thing is fixed in my memory, I remember very little of the Andy/Fergie event. Apart, that is, from a moment of panic as I entered the abbey. It occurred to me at the first royal wedding that, no matter how sparkling your prose, an event such as this is always going to be dominated by the sights, sounds and colour that TV does so much better than newspapers. I had to reach the senses that telly couldn't touch. Scent – of course! I would bring to our readers the entwined odours of a million (guesstimate) wedding blooms. I would create a word-sniff of heady hyacinth, gorgeous gardenias and sultry sage. Inside the abbey, I inhaled deeply to fill my senses with the olfactory delights I would share with the readers. Westminster Abbey smelt of absolutely nothing. It was utterly neutral, devoid of the merest suggestion of any scent. So I wrote something about the mischievous page boys instead. Not my finest hour.

The Charles and Di saga ended in August 1997 when that speeding Mercedes hurtled into a concrete pillar in a Paris underpass. The world gasped in disbelief and Britain prepared to bury a saint. I was detailed to cover the princess's funeral, not from Westminster Abbey but among the crowds lining the route. Fate and some dodgy seafood gave me a rare perspective on the events of the day.

I was staying with the Editor and women's editor at a hotel in Westminster, sharing a twin room with the boss. On the day before the funeral we walked among the crowds as they settled in for the night. In situations like this there is only one way to find the people you want to interview. You have to ask. The veteran foreign correspondent Edward Behr witnessed a reporter doing this routine with hideous insensitivity among the shattered European survivors of the 1950s Belgian Congo atrocities, repeatedly asking the queue: "Anyone here been raped and speaks English?" (That question became the title of his autobiography but was deemed unacceptable in America where the book was re-titled blandly: "Bearings: A Foreign Correspondent's Life Behind the Lines").

In the streets of Westminster we began our sing-song appeal: "Anyone here from the West Midlands? Anyone read the Express & Star?" Within a few minutes we had a dozen Black Country folk, all eager to talk about their love for Diana and, in some cases, their disdain for the House of Windsor. It sometimes comes as a surprise how little respect for the monarchy is held by many ordinary people. I recall an old soldiers' pilgrimage to Cyprus shortly before Charles married Camilla in April 2005. The men in their regimental blazers and their wives in floaty, old-fashioned summer frocks, seemed the epitome of loyal English folk. Until the conversation turned to Charles.

"Remind me again," said one sweet 60-something lady, "when exactly is that bat-eared idiot getting married?"

For hundreds of reporters, covering Diana's funeral was essentially a static job. You were either locked in Westminster Abbey or stuck in the million-strong crush outside, unable to move left or right. I had a different perspective, thanks to my choice from the menu the night before. If I have a golden rule of journalism it is to avoid seafood. So at this dinner in a smart hotel with the editor and women's editor, I glanced at the menu and ordered what I took to be lamb. Good, safe stuff, lamb. When it arrived I discovered I had ordered not escalope but scallops, which the dictionary describes as an edible bivalve mollusc and my alimentary system described as something horrendous to be ejected from the body as quickly as possible. At 3am I was vomiting and suffering extreme diarrhoea, never an easy balancing act. By 4am, purged and feeling fine, I rose, showered, dressed and plunged out of the hotel and into the thickening crowds in Whitehall.

My intention was to find a good spot, maybe somewhere in the Mall. In the event I walked the entire length of the funeral procession, from Westminster Abbey to Kensington Palace, chatting with little groups of people on the way. Some were sombre but, at that stage, I saw no-one sobbing. Later, some of our photographers admitted they had to work hard to find any evidence of tears, even as the princess's coffin passed by. Every picture desk wanted "Britain in Tears" images but that was not the real mood of the moment. Rather, I found people doing what Brits always do at such times. They were chatting, joking, taking photos of each other. One group had even brought a table and piled it with food and drink. The mood in that section, although not raucous, was more carnival than funeral.

I squeezed myself against some railings near the palace and we all waited. And then it happened. It was the strangest sensation. Suddenly, above the hubbub of the crowd, you heard a distant tinkling of horse brasses and the low growl of the gun-carriage wheels on asphalt. All talking ceased. It was as though someone had laid a huge, sound-proof blanket over the people and only the rattle of the carriage could be heard. It swept past. There was a fleeting glimpse of the flag-draped coffin topped with lilies and I had a momentary vision of Diana's face inside the coffin, at rest. I have attended dozens of funerals and never experienced anything like that moment.

As the coffin passed, the chatter resumed and I made my way to Hyde Park where the crowds were gathering in the sunshine for the big-screen transmission from the Abbey. I did something I rarely do, dictating my report straight into a mobile phone without making any notes. Across the park, London was deserted. I hailed a taxi to Euston, got straight on a train to Coventry and was back home in Warwickshire as Elton John was singing "Candle in the Wind."

Royalty is a strange thing. It barely affects our democracy and it rarely touches our lives. And yet the attention it commands is extraordinary. I recall two visits to the Express & Star offices. The first was Michael Heseltine, then deputy prime minister and a vital cog in the wheels of government. He arrived at Wolverhampton station, chatted freely with people in the streets as he walked to the office, did his interview with me and a photographer and then did an unscheduled walkabout in the city centre, pressing the flesh. I am sure he had personal security but I couldn't see it.

Compare and contrast Hezza's easy, informal visit with that of the Prince of Wales in the same year. Days before the visit, armed detectives arrived to check out the building for exits, entrances and hiding places. In the hours before the prince arrived, a second police posse descended, this time with some eager springer spaniels trained to detect explosives. They bounced cheerfully around the office for a few minutes. And then one of those spaniels, from several yards away, suddenly sniffed the air and made a beeline for my desk. He sat down, tail wagging frantically with his nose against my top drawer. His handler joined him, followed by the deputy editor who was looking alarmed.

"Do you mind if I look?" said the handler indicating the drawer.

"Can I just say," I replied, "that it is a very small quantity, for my personal use?"

The officer laughed. I smiled. The deputy editor, who had no sense of humour and obviously thought the dog had found a drugs stash, looked terrified. I opened the drawer. This highly trained springer spaniel had detected neither gelignite nor cannabis. It was a Twix bar.

The police check was finished and HRH duly arrived. I'm not sure if he remembers the building or the newspaper. What really grabbed his attention was the editorial librarian Fran who was wearing a dramatic, low-cut royal blue number for the occasion. But I never understood why the security was so relaxed for an important government minister with matchless experience and contacts who could be described as irreplaceable, and yet so tight for the Windsor heir who, if he suddenly died, would be instantly replaced by the next in line with barely a ripple in the system.

An invitation to the Palace

In 1981 Prince Philip, Duke of Edinburgh, became President of the World Wildlife Fund. Over the following years he emerged as a global spokesman for conservation and in 1987 the WWF changed its name to the World Wide Fund for Nature.

"We ought to speak to him," Keith Parker, editor of the Express & Star declared one morning in 1988 after the daily conference. We minions nodded obediently.

Parker never lacked confidence in his newspaper. As far as he was concerned it was right up there with the giants of Fleet Street. Which meant that if any of the great and good were suddenly elected, or promoted, no matter how famous, they would obviously be desperately keen to talk about it to an evening newspaper in Wolverhampton. A growing pile of polite refusals, notably from the Prince of Wales to whom we made several approaches over many years, told another story.

We could certainly write to Buckingham Palace and crave an audience with Prince Philip but it was generally agreed that the chances of getting it would be about as rare as a giant panda in Peckham.

To our astonishment, the Duke of Edinburgh replied that he would be delighted to talk to us for an hour one morning in July. He didn't want a photographer to be present but apart from that one stipulation, this was a no-rules encounter. He didn't want great detail about the questions to be asked and there was no stipulation on copy approval, headlines or photographs to be used. Furthermore, this interview at Buckingham Palace was taking place at the height of the IRA guerilla campaign. It is worth stressing a simple point: media interviews with such celebrities on such relaxed terms simply do not happen. Why the Duke agreed to the E&S interview is anyone's guess, although we heard later that one of his foreign trips had been cancelled and he had a couple of free days. He could have gone racing or carriage riding. Instead, he chatted to us.

After an exchange of letters on security issues, I reported on a July morning in 1988 to the privy door at Buckingham Palace. Two security officials manned a desk.

"And you are?"

"I'm from the Express & Star in Wolverhampton. I have come to interview the Duke of Edinburgh."

"Ah, yes," said one official, consulting his list. "So you must be Mr Parker."

"No."

"What, you're not Mr Parker?"

"No, I'm not. He's the editor. My name is Rhodes." For a grisly moment I saw the entire operation collapsing over a silly miscommunication, and me being sent back to Wolverhampton with an empty notebook and tail between legs.

"Ah, well," said the security officer genially. "I'm sure it'll be all right," and after checking my bag he waved me through.

I was shown to a ground-floor ante-room where two Gurkha officers were sitting, presumably expecting an audience, both looking nervous. The fireplace was an old fashioned double radiant-bar device with revolving discs creating a flame effect. Above it hung Ford Madox Brown's 1855 painting, The Last of England with its two emigrants gazing glumly as they set off for a new life in America. Whether it was the original, a watercolour replica or a print I know not but the décor of that little room was more Home Counties middle-class than palatial. An aide led me up the red and gold staircase to the Duke's private study and the great man entered, followed by a servant bearing a tray with coffee and biscuits. Prince Philip himself (and this is the story I will tell my grandchildren) poured the coffee. He was relaxed and affable, a striking figure in a pale grey suit with a tie in a large knot. I resisted the temptation to ask if it were a Windsor knot. And away we went, talking about everything wildlife-related, from a virus killing seals in the North Sea to the long-term effects of deforestation. More than 20 years after the interview, I played the tape and his words were prescient. In 1988 he knew what the 21st century might bring.

He was not an easy interview. I began by using one of his own quotes from a national newspaper and he demanded, with a smile, to see my evidence. I produced the cutting.

And when I raised the vexed issue of how a man like him, speaking up for wildlife could possibly shoot game birds, he seemed quite unprepared and, for a moment, riled.

"Well, that's like saying adultery is all right so long as you don't enjoy it, isn't it?" he snapped. I'm not sure it was but I didn't pursue the matter. I'm glad we got the interview. It made two big leader-page features for the Express & Star and Keith Parker was delighted.

"So what sort of person is he?" Parker asked me the day after the interview. I thought about it.

"The sort of person," I replied, "who very rarely hears the word 'no'."

Like father, like daughter. I interviewed Princess Anne at the launch of a charity's promotional film in the 1990s. After the screening she stood alone, unsmiling. Protocol dictates that, when it comes to royals, you speak only when you are spoken to. But then protocol doesn't have a 600-word gap to fill on the next day's Express & Star in Wolverhampton, and I did. So I went across to her and asked whether she'd enjoyed the film. Not much, it transpired. The Princess Royal does not sugar-coat things. No, she did not care for the film. And why not? "Where are all the black faces?" Anne demanded. She made the point that this charity employed local staff and supporters in Africa, yet the film showed only the white British organisers. This must have been the beginning of the turning against the "white saviour" view of the world in which black and brown people are portrayed as helpless recipients of aid from wise and generous white folk. Like her father, her views were ahead of the time.

But she also has a sense of humour, as I learned from a sergeant involved in the planning of a visit by the Princess Royal to the Royal Corps of Signals training regiment at Catterick. A 12ft square frame tent containing a chemical toilet had been erected on the training area for the sole use of the princess. To his horror, the quartermaster realised it was too far from the mobile generators to provide lighting. He dispatched a team of squaddies to the stores to gather hundreds of standard-issue green torches which were hung by string from the roof of the tent to illuminate the loo.

HRH duly arrived, inspected the troops and used the facility. As she emerged she smiled and remarked: "It's like a fairy grotto, isn't it?"

From Cov to Brum to Wolves

I joined the Evening Mail in Birmingham soon after the Royal Wedding in 1981, following a strange phone call from the editor. Keith Whetstone, my former boss at Coventry, had been editor of the Evening Mail for some months and wanted me to join him in Birmingham as a feature writer and columnist.

His chief feature writer and leader writer, Maurice Rotheroe, was a gifted journalist. But his first love was fungi. Rotheroe was destined to become one of the world's greatest experts on mushrooms and toadstools. It was an all-consuming passion and the day came when, in the battle between features and fungi, fungi won. Rotheroe left the Evening Mail and I took his place.

For the first couple of years I loved everything about the Evening Mail. It was selling a quarter-of-a-million copies a night and was a big, confident institution in the Second City. Everybody knew the Evening Mail and "Mailman Rhodes" with his Rhodes on Monday column became well-known on the patch. It was the Evening Mail that sent me on my first big foreign assignment, to Hong Kong. The travel editor said he'd love to go himself but shortly before he'd experienced a forced-landing in an airliner and it put him off flying for good.

But in the mid 80s things began to change. The Evening Mail features department was merged with that of the Birmingham Post. The Post, an upmarket broadsheet, was reduced to the same tabloid size as the Evening Mail. This made perfect sense to the accountants because it meant news, feature and advertisement pages could be shared between the two newspapers. This overlooked the simple fact that the Evening Mail was a working-class read and the Post was much posher; it liked to think of itself as "influential." The result of the page-sharing was that horny-handed Evening Mail readers, expecting human-interest features, were presented with arcane articles on Lalique glassware or the story of the Ballet Russe while middle-class Post readers were opening their paper to find rather vulgar fashions modelled by footballers' girlfriends.

I was gradually drawn out of writing and into admin, promotions and competitions which was tedious. I stayed only because the colleagues were great company.

Fred Norris, the showbiz editor, was a legend. He had a wonderful fund of yarns told in a deliciously dry way. During the war he had been a teenage fire-watcher in Birmingham and, like so many blitz veterans, was horrified at the damage done to his beloved city not only by German bombs but by fragments of British anti-aircraft shells falling to earth.

"We had this arrangement with the Jerries," Fred explained. "They'd send over a spotter plane and we'd wreck the city."

It was Fred Norris who, fed up with interviews over meals when the chat disrupted the eating, and vice versa, introduced a miniature tape-recorder into the system. He was due to interview Jacqueline Bisset in a smart hotel and knew that, as he'd be taking a constant shorthand note, he wouldn't enjoy the meal. So he wired himself for sound, the tape-recorder in his pocket and the microphone taped to his left wrist. There was no subterfuge; the actress knew what was happening and she and Fred enjoyed their lunch. Back at the office, disaster. As Fred played back the tape, you could dimly discern a deep male voice (his) and a high female voice (hers). But the words were entirely drowned out by a staccato, insistent tic-tic-tic. Fred had successfully recorded an hour of his own wristwatch.

In 1985 an advert appeared in the UK Press Gazette for a "Top Writer" at the Express & Star in Wolverhampton. The vacancy arose on the sudden death of Ray Seaton, a long-serving and cherished member of the Express & Star writing team. I knew Ray, having met him on a veterans' pilgrimage to Arnhem in the 1980s. Together we joined a party of old Paras as they trudged the route from Osterbeke down to the River Rhine where in 1944 they had slipped away after the disastrous "Bridge Too Far" operation. It was a raw, cold night for the old chaps and by the time we reached the river many an ex-soldier was sniffing. On pilgrimages such as this you always uncover some new nugget of unrecorded history. The accepted version of the end of the Arnhem battle is that the British troops vanished silently, undetected by the eagle-eyed Germans. One old soldier had a different take on it. His view was that the Germans were more concerned with keeping dry than machine-gunning a defeated enemy. He told us: "I think it was the rain that saved us more than anything. The Germans hated it as much as we did."

The day over, Ray and I retired to the hotel in Eindhoven where, to save money, we shared a room. There was the usual awkwardness that goes with such arrangements. Ray was a neat room mate, folding his clothes into precise squares and laying them out on shelves in the bathroom. He insisted I should use the shower first. I ran both taps to get the right temperature then flicked the switch for the shower. I have never seen water pressure like it. The vertical shower hose suddenly stiffened like a living thing. The shower head flew off its mounting and thrashed around the bathroom like an anaconda with a seizure, drenching the room and washing Ray's neat piles of vests and Y-fronts on to the floor. Entirely unruffled, Ray Seaton sat on the edge of the bath wringing out his smalls and smilingly observed that such things happen. A gentleman.

The city slickers of the Evening Mail tended to look down on the E&S, a brash little tabloid with not even a city base. It circulated in the towns of the Black Country to the west of Brum and, for all the sneering, was technologically way ahead of the Post & Mail, having its own computer system and software company. More to the point, its daily circulation was already matching the Evening Mail and would soon overtake it.

The technology was an attraction. At some stage in the 1980s, most journalists experienced the culture-shock of what we used to call the new technology. The setting of words in type, an ancient craft conducted for decades by grumpy old printers operating the typewriter-from-hell known as the Linotype, was taken over by computers. Newsrooms which once clattered to the racket of dozens of typewriters, and the oaths of printers dropping slabs of print, fell silent. Offices became calm, quiet and carpeted. Work stations were grouped in little oases of potted plants. The grumpy old men either re-trained as sub-editors or vanished. In 1981 I attended a technology conference in Brighton where the latest computer technology aimed at what was increasingly called The Media was on display. At lunch I found myself sitting next to someone I vaguely knew from the printing works in Brum.

"So what do you do?" I asked chummily.

"Me?" he sighed. "I'm a dinosaur. A bloody dinosaur."

Nobody I know captured the change better than Gerry Anderson, a columnist at the Express & Star who was a legend in the Black Country. This is how he put it:

"The transition from hot metal to cold technology in the newspaper world was more than what cosmologists like to call 'a quantum leap'. Certainly in production terms it was that, but for journalists and composing-room staff it was something akin to major surgery of the soul. It was like waking up to discover that a magic you had not previously given full credit had walked out on you and all the old, familiar sounds had been replaced by a clinical, sterile silence."

The E&S had a fascinating history, being founded in the 1880s by a group of radical Liberals in the town, including a local butcher Thomas Graham, financed by one of the richest men in the world, the Scottish-American industrialist Andrew Carnegie. He created "Carnegie's Echoes," a string of regional newspapers from Sunderland in the north to Portsmouth in the south. His aim was the creation of the British Republic, on the lines of the United States, with Queen Victoria packed off back to Germany. The Echoes' manifesto – abolition of the monarchy, home rule for Ireland, scrapping the House of Lords and creating a republic – horrified the British Establishment but came to nothing as Victoria's popularity grew in the final decades of the 19th century. In 1902 Carnegie broke his links with the Express & Star which passed into the hands of the Graham Family.

I answered the advert and landed the job. And there I stayed, in various forms from 1985 to the present. The Express & Star sent me around the world to see places I'd never dreamed of and to meet people I would never otherwise have encountered. The best of moves.

Honestly, everything's just fine

The very best foreign assignments are the ones organised by governments eager to tell the world that, honestly, everything's just fine. You are an honoured guest. You are flown business or even first-class. You are met at the airport and your luggage is whisked away by flunkies. You are plied with fine wine and excellent food. You are introduced to senior politicians and officials who smile a lot.

There are two snags to this arrangement, the first for you and the second for your hosts. The problem for the hack is the knowledge that, no matter how it's dressed up, you are being employed as a propagandist, although in my experience good journalists keep their objectivity no matter who is picking up the bill. The problem for your hosts is that, time and again, the moment they have assured you that everything's just fine, it stops being fine. It really is uncanny.

Sri Lanka 1983, everything fine

A party of national and provincial reporters was invited to visit the island, ostensibly as guests of the national carrier Air Lanka but actually the government in Colombo, to assure the world that the latest civil strife was nothing to worry about. The truth was that a civil war was beginning that would last

26 years and eventually claim up to 100,000 lives. Really, everything's just fine.

It had started a few weeks before our arrival with ambushes and random killings of Tamils by Sinhalese and vice versa. The first night in Colombo was uneventful but as we headed north a couple of days later, we met a couple of army convoys of jeeps, troop lorries and armoured cars. That evening we passed through a village where everything was far from fine. Huddled groups stood at street corners, their belonging tied into parcels with sheets. Burned-out houses smoked. Two nights later we moved to the old colonial Hotel Suisse in Kandy. A couple of us walked out that evening and were approached by an anxious middle-aged man.

"You are the journalists?" he asked. "The English journalists?"

We had no idea anyone in the town knew we were coming but we introduced ourselves. He beckoned us towards a drainage ditch running in front of his house. The surface looked oily.

This, he explained with tears welling was where his friend and neighbour who had lived in the town for many years had been hacked to pieces by a gang. We were looking at a puddle of blood and body fluids. How had it happened? Why? He could not answer. But as with so many civil wars, the answer was probably that the victim had the wrong name or the wrong god.

The ghastly irony was that while this shell-shocked man was showing us a murder scene, life in beautiful, tourist-thronged Kandy was bubbling like champagne. We haggled for carved coconut elephants and yards of sari silk in the vast market. We took a sunset boat ride across the sacred lake with big, fat gouramis kissing at the surface. I cannot think of a more blissful evening yet the madness, like a mind-eating pandemic, was taking root.

Our guide was a tall, distinguished gentleman called Stanley who loved the English and their literature. At Nuwara Eliya in the high, tea-growing part of Sri Lanka, Stanley introduced the press party to the Hill Club, a bastion of the Raj where, in days long past, British subalterns haggled over their mess bills and, according to the yellowing comments book under a glass screen, denounced the local laundry boys in language that would have shamed Kipling. It was an impressive room, flanked with hunting trophies and oozing imperial confidence.

"Well," I remarked, "this is another fine mess you've got us into, Stanley."

Stanley looked shocked, then puzzled. Then his face broke into a huge smile. "Ah, yes," he said. "A fine mess – Laurel and Hardy." And then, using the excellent acoustics of the hall, he spontaneously delivered a few lines from Shakespeare: "The quality of mercy is not strained; It droppeth as the gentle rain from heaven. Upon the place beneath."

And I asked Stanley what had happened to mercy on this beautiful, blessed island of his. Why were neighbours, all following religions that preached peace, hacking each other to pieces and burning down villages?

His expression changed, first to sadness and then to a flash of pure panic and dread for the future.

"I do not know, Peter. I simply do not know."

South Africa 1986, everything fine

In January 1986 the E&S assistant editor Roy Coates sidled conspiratorially over to my desk and, checking we were alone, asked quietly: "Peter, would you have any moral objections to going to South Africa for us for a week?"

My moral dilemma last almost a nano-second. As I may have said earlier, when it comes to foreign assignments what matters is not how you get there or who picks up the bill but what you write. South Africa during apartheid was a pariah state and the press trip being offered was unashamedly an advertising exercise for South African tourism. They would show us what they wanted us to see and there would be not a hope of digging deep into the politics of the place. And yet I wanted to be there. I wanted to see this regime before it vanished into history. I also wanted to go on safari.

I stayed overnight at Heathrow. In the hotel bar I found myself next to a chatty young bloke with a blonde pageboy hairstyle wearing an orange one-piece jump suit. I bought him a drink and we talked.

"So what do you do?" I asked.

"I'm in a rock band."

This was dangerous territory for me. My music was of the Sixties and Seventies. In the 1980s I was totally immersed in work and the TA. I could recognise most regimental marches but the pop and rock revolution of that decade passed me by.

"A band I might have heard of?" I ventured.

"Black Sabbath," he smiled.

It was some years later that I realised I'd been sharing stories with Ozzy Osbourne. Journalists meet celebrities all the time but the ground rules are clear and you both know the time, date and purpose of your interview. There is always a special thrill in simply bumping in to the rich and famous by chance, just as Joe Public would do.

I had a similar unplanned encounter in the days when I was a district reporter in Stratford-upon-Avon. I was invited to the Shakespeare Festival luncheon, a grand affair in a huge marquee where tickets seemed to have been distributed randomly. There was no press table; we hacks were scattered among the actors, ambassadors and local politicians at this great annual event. I found myself sitting next to a cheerful little Yorkshireman. Two Tykes together, we chatted merrily through lunch. It was only later that I realised he was J B Priestley.

I flew out of Heathrow for South Africa in 14F degrees of frost. When I had parked my car the day before, a tiny weasel had shot underneath it, seeking the warmth of a hot engine. We landed at Johannesburg at 114F and boarded a light plane to Kruger national park. Transferring to a minibus, I caught my first glimpse of African fauna.

"Bloody hell!" I exclaimed. "Look, it's an ostrich!" The huge bird was running alongside the vehicle.

"There's another!" yelled a fellow hack on the six-strong party.

"And another," shouted someone else. "Look, there's bloody hundreds of ostriches!"

The African driver turned round with the voice of calm.

"Sir, the reason there are lots of ostriches is that this is an ostrich farm."

Kruger was every wildlife documentary you'd ever seen, rolled into one 48-hour experience. We counted 140 species of birds and animals from tiny mongooses, pouring in their thousands across the track like a grey tidal wave, to 100-strong groups of elephants. We suddenly understood, as you can never understand in zoos or safari parks in England, how camouflage works. You find yourself wondering why that tree is moving. Look again and it's a giraffe. We came across a mother cheetah with four or five young. In the dappled shade of a thorn bush you could just make them out. But as she saw the approaching Land-Rovers and their cargo of humans, she led her kittens away. That feline family simply vanished. It was as though mother and young had been turned into one big silk scarf, lazily waving in the sunlight and shadows, the individual creatures impossible to see. The elephants looked harmless. Our guide told us that only a week ago a tourist from Switzerland, assuming they were like the tame zoo elephants back home, left his car and offered a bun to an elephant.

"What was left of him was hardly worth putting in a coffin," said the guide.

Most impressive of all was the creature who came loping down the road, alone and unafraid, high at the front, low at the back as if permanently walking uphill and with a big smile that sometimes turns into a laugh. Lord of his domain and as ugly as sin, the hyena passed by.

We had a memorable evening meal in Kruger at a camp station smelling of blossom and hot sand. The guides set up a couple of tables, lit the hurricane lamps at twilight and served a banquet of huge braised steaks which may or may not have been elephant. Those hurricane lamps were a mistake, acting as a beacon for every flying insect for miles around. The swarm of moths, beetles and God-knows-what crashing into us and our lanterns grew worse. Finally something the size of a sparrow smacked into a woman reporter's bosom and she screamed. The lamps were put on a nearby table, the swarm of insects changed their flight path and we settled down to the meal, undisturbed. But not for long. A few hundred yards away, as is often the case in Africa, something began killing and eating something else. It was a pitiful performance. We couldn't see into the ebony blackness; we could only imagine the horror behind the noise.

"Grrrr," roared the predator, probably a lion or leopard, in a deep growl.

"Weak, weak," went its prey in a falsetto cry.

"Grrr."

"Weak, weak."

And so it went on for 20 frightful minutes, the growls growing deeper and more satisfied as the beast tasted blood, the weak-weak growing fainter and more desperate. At first our sympathies were entirely with the prey species, probably some beautiful, photogenic little antelope. Damn and blast that wicked big cat. But as the death throes continued, the mood changed. Impatience spread.

"Oh, for God's sake, just die," said one of the hacks. He spoke for us all.

Safari was an unforgettable experience. But out on the veldt we were never going to discover much about South Africa. Our hosts, fit young white lads, talked freely about their hopes for the future and said they would have no problem working for black bosses. But we were kept well away from any blacks, partly by distance but also by the cultural problem of a white foreigner approaching a black citizen and the black man knowing that he may have to explain the conversation to his white boss. You cannot simply stick your nose in without thinking of the consequences.

At a beach near Cape Town our hosts took pains to show us the wicked old symbols of apartheid. The beach signs declaring: "White area" had been painted over. What they couldn't explain was why the signs were still in place. If you're serious about equal rights you don't merely paint over the old signs, you rip them down.

In a neat move in the hotel that night, one of the women reporters excused herself and slipped away for a few minutes.

She encountered a black maid collecting the bedding and simply asked what the maid thought of her life.

"The whites have so much and we have so little," replied the maid. Ten little words said more about South Africa in 1986 than any number of signs, painted out or otherwise. I included that quote in my tourism feature. And then something unexpected happened. The UN sanctions on South Africa were strengthened to include all sorts of trade issues plus anything that might promote tourism in the state. So my safari articles and photographs were filed away in the E&S electronic archive until the rules changed. And that is where they stayed for the next six years until 1992 when, as the road to democracy began to open, sanctions were eased and a new era began.

Israel 1987, everything fine

This was a media trip organised by an agency of the Israeli government to convince the world that everything was just fine. Israel was frantically trying to burnish its image after its invasion of Lebanon five years earlier which ended hideously with the Sabra and Shatila massacres. By a miracle of bad timing our press party landed at Tel Aviv just as things stopped being fine, a couple of days after what every Palestinian calls the Night of the Gliders.

It was an audacious attack. Two fighters of the Palestine Liberation Organisation (PLO) flew into northern Israel on hang-gliders and killed six Israeli soldiers. The Palestinians in the occupied West Bank were ecstatic; their riots turned into the first Intifada. The Israelis were shocked and humiliated.

And so our first unscheduled appointment in Jerusalem was an impromptu briefing where a senior Israeli official outlined sadly what had happened. Then the strangest thing happened. The official said: "I suppose you want to hear the PLO view on this?" Puzzled, we agreed and a mini-bus was summoned. It took us across Jerusalem to the offices of the PLO where a Palestinian spokesman gleefully described the killings as a great operation and praised the bravery of the slain PLO fighters.

It was bizarre. This was the equivalent of the British Army, at the height of the Troubles in Northern Ireland, giving reporters a lift across Belfast to interview the Provisional IRA. To this day, I have no idea why the Israelis felt they had to provide a platform for their enemies. A very odd sort of night.

The Israel trip, coinciding with the Night of the Gliders and increased security, turned into a curious blend of tourism and defence issues. We descended to the Dead Sea which then, as now, was actually several seas owing to the drop in water level caused by massive abstraction from the River Jordan upstream. We floated uncertainly in the slippery brine and I was photographed in the classic attitude, reclining on my back while wearing a straw hat and reading a copy of the Express & Star.

"How have you got a copy of your paper out here?" demanded one of the other hacks. I explained that I had brought it with me for this very moment, which he seemed to regard as unfair. I also managed to fall out with one of the women reporters in the party who wanted to know why the men could swim in the Dead Sea but the women were instantly flipped on to their backs by the super-buoyant water. I explained as delicately as I could that I'd read somewhere that it was due to the difference in fat distribution in men and women.

"You sexist pig!" she snarled. There are times when it is wise to act thick and keep your mouth shut.

On the way back to Jerusalem we spotted a couple of big black Bedouin tents among the sand dunes of the desert. After some cajoling our guide, a former Israeli para who had grown up among Arabs and spoke Arabic fluently, made his way to the settlement. After a couple of minutes he beckoned us over. The Bedouin women were ushered out of sight into one tent while the old, bearded patriarch invited us into the bigger tent, carpeted with an ancient rug, and introduced us to his son and grandson. This was not on the agenda. Our guide was surprised that we would want to meet these tent-dwellers but the Bedouins seemed delighted these British visitors had dropped in as they poured scented tea into an assortment of old china cups and glasses. We didn't stay long and we didn't discuss anything of great import. But their dress told a fascinating tale. The old man was wearing his full black robe with an ancient Western waistcoat beneath. His son was in the familiar uniform of guerillas and rebels everywhere, a battered set of US Army green combat fatigues. The grandson was wearing shorts and an American T-shirt and would have looked instantly at home in New York or Denver. Anyone might draw the conclusion that this ancient way of life was being subsumed, in just three generations, into the all-embracing fashions and mind-set of the West. How wrong that would be. The intifada was under way and the son of that little boy in the American T-shirt would probably grow up not envying or admiring the USA but hating it.

And on to the Golan Heights, captured from Syria during the 1973 Yom Kippur War. In the heat and dust of the evening, an Israeli tank battalion showed off its Israel-built Merkava tanks on a vast plain. Their heavy machine gun fire sent flickering lines of tracer bouncing into the distance as the sun went down over the Sea of Galilee and cicadas hummed all around.

On our final day we visited Yad Vashem in Jerusalem, the museum of the Holocaust. It produced this column:

Jerusalem, December 1987

Calvary was all incense and icons. Bethlehem was traffic jams and tatty tourist trash. Some may find God there but, for me, it was as unmoving and meaningless as seeking Arthurian legend in Woolworths. And yet Israel can suddenly flay your emotions, usually when you least expect it. As when we met the children of a kibbutz on the northern border. Tiny tots singing songs and rehearsing the school play, too young to be aware that their classroom was a gas-proofed bomb shelter. Or when I talked to a nurse who tries to patch up the damage when little minds like these are torn and shattered by the sudden shriek and thump of terrorist rockets. And, of course, there was Yad Vashem, the Holocaust Museum in Jerusalem where the Nazis' efficient, businesslike, almost emotionless destruction of six million souls is recorded. The pictures are harrowing. Naked men and women standing at the edge of a pit full of bodies, waiting their turn to be shot. A giant of a man in a Lithuanian street, bludgeoning Jews to death with an iron bar. A street in Warsaw after the Jews had been carted off to the death camps. Pathetic bundles of clothes and suitcases left behind by the kerb.

Most poignantly of all, a tiny tot of three or four in a hand-me-down coat and outsize Andy Capp hat being led by his mother to the gas chamber. As innocent and unsuspecting as my own toddler when I lead her to the bath and I know it is hair-wash night and she does not.

There is also a new memorial, to the Children of the Holocaust. How in God's name do you commemorate 1,500,000 children? At Yad Vashem photographs of just a handful of the dead gaze out of the gloom, framed by four huge candles. You walk past into a vast, seemingly infinite, pitch-black place where mirror upon mirror make endless reflections of the flickering lights. It is like moving through a galaxy, surrounded by millions of tiny sparks that twinkled briefly before being snuffed out forever at Auschwitz, Dachau and the rest.

Some hours later I arrived home in England to find my daughter standing on the kitchen dresser, face against the window, squealing with excitement. I had planned a homecoming of laughter but there is something very potent in the baby-powder softness of a tiny child, something that triggered all those images of kids in bunkers, bundles at the kerbside and a toddler in an Andy Capp hat. I held her close and cradled her head.

The Maldives 2004, everything not quite fine

On Boxing Day 2004 a tsunami swept across south-east Asia, killing more than 220,000 people and devastating cities, towns and entire islands. The Maldives were not the worst-affected of places but more than 100 people died, half the capital Male was inundated and two-thirds of the islands-state's GDP was wiped out. A few weeks after the disaster, in February 2005, the Maldives government organised a media party from Britain to persuade UK holidaymakers that the islands were open for business. In short, everything was fine. In truth, it pretty much was. None of the feared after-shocks had appeared, the resorts were open, if half-empty, and the

Maldivians on the tourist islands seemed in good spirits. More to the point, the Brits had returned to the Maldives in huge numbers, long before most other Western nations took the plunge. Maybe the Brits are unusually brave. Or maybe they lack imagination.

According to one resort manager, the Tsunami revealed clear cultural differences. He recalled how, after the tsunami burst over the island the terrified residents reacted in distinct national ways to the threat of a second wave. The French climbed on to the chalet roofs. The English climbed into the trees. But the fatalistic, organised Germans huddled in the tennis court so that, if the worst happened, their bodies would be held in the high wire-mesh fencing and recovered. In the same resort, but staying in an offshore chalet on stilts safely above the water level, a pair of tourists paddled over to the stricken island. They explained to the drenched, shell-shocked residents that they were psychotherapists, and did anyone need counselling? The manager said it was curious how "f**k off" sounds the same in so many languages.

It was a memorably lavish press trip. We were whisked from island to island in speedboats and seaplanes and accommodated in the finest cabins. But the fear of the tsunami returning was ever-present, even when we sat out in the golden evenings sipping our gin slings, and huge, leathery-winged fruit bats flapped overhead. The more imminent threat was death by coconut. Every year a handful of people across the tropics are killed by coconuts dropping 40 feet or more to the ground. In the still of the night you could hear the impacts, thump, thump. Our hosts were more than generous and would not accept our money for anything. This was fortunate because I had packed £100 in cash and spent £90 of it on phone charges the first night fruitlessly trying to make a UK connection with my new and unfamiliar Apple laptop. When I finally got it working, I filed a series of features entitled "After the Tsunami." And while they were generally upbeat, the penultimate day took us to a place where hope seemed to have vanished. It was a tiny island where the community and their ancestors had lived safe and peaceful lives for many centuries on a diet of coconuts, fish and crystal-clear water from their well.

And then the tsunami struck. In a matter of seconds the wall of water swept over the island. In her workshop, a block-built cabin with an ancient Singer sewing machine against one wall, a woman explained how the water burst in under her door and rose in the hut until it was about six inches from the ceiling; the tide mark on the wall was still visible. For a few frantic seconds she was trapped under water and expected to drown. And then the tsunami vanished as quickly as it had come. People hunted for their loved ones and, for a few minutes, all seemed well. And then they realised three children of the village were missing. One little body was found a few hours later but the other two were swept out into the sea. The children had gone, the crops were ruined, some houses were wrecked and their faithful wells were fouled with salt water. On the day we arrived, it was reassuring to see big, sturdy UN tents providing good accommodation. But there was a sense of despair, of old certainties lost. Now their beloved island, self-sufficient for so many years, was kept alive by daily deliveries of fresh water in tankers, and no-one knew how long this could go on. And among all the other worries, the big one. If the tsunami came once, might it come again? And when?

Hong Kong – security alert

I was lucky with Hong Kong. I worked there on four occasions, first in 1982, twice in 1993 and finally in 1996 in the build-up to the Territory being handed over by HM Government to the People's Republic of China. I loved the place. It was beguiling, eternally dazzling with a surprise around every corner. As I wrote after one business meeting:

High in his air-conditioned office, surrounded by maps and plans, David could be in any Western city. Down below in the crazy, jostling side-streets of Wan Chai is the unchanging Orient. A few yards from the office door, the snake man is setting out his stall. To the half-amused interest of passers-by, he selects a snake from the writhing basket at his feet. He decapitates it with a knife, slits open its protesting belly and expertly extracts the gall-bladder, a prized and reputedly powerful aphrodisiac. Snake heads litter the pavement like ancient Celtic jewellery, sightless eyes gazing up as the mirrored skyscrapers glint in the sun.

The biggest surprise was the way HK kept on growing. In 1982 I peeked over the frontier to Red China to see two bored-looking guards, a shed and a small warehouse. Nine years later it had become a city.

In my first trip we took a boat to the Royal Hong Kong Yacht Club on an island in the bay. By the next visit the island had become part of the mainland as HK's eternal dredging and land-reclamation marched onwards. In 1993 I took a ride on a speed boat with a public-relations lady from the new airport project. To make a place for the airport, the enterprising Brits and Chinese were simply lopping the top off a mountain and smearing it into the South China Sea. Job done.

"When I tell my mother in China I am in public relations," she told me in halting English, "she very angry. She thought public relations means prostitute."

That's one for the PR industry to debate.

I never used the new airport. My four flights in and out of HK all involved the old Kai Tak airport which one pilot described to me as "so dangerous that they never have accidents." The approach and landing, over the rooftops of apartment blocks so close you felt you could touch them, demanded extreme skill and caution. For pilots it was a challenge, for visitors an unforgettable experience. A Chinese lady looked up from hanging out her washing as our Boeing glided over. I swear I could see her smile.

My first assignment was as a guest of HK Government to write a business supplement on investment opportunities in the colony (or territory, as they preferred to call it). It began in confusion. There were just two of us on this press trip, me for the Birmingham Post and a Scottish reporter, let us call him Mac, for the Scotsman newspaper in Edinburgh.

It was a 13-hour flight, luxury Marco Polo-class and an empty seat next to me suggested that Mac had missed the flight. So as the hundreds of passengers poured off, I positioned myself at the entrance to Kai Tak arrivals, looking out for a Scottish journalist. It was a motley assortment, mostly Chinese but with a scattering of Brits in various stages of dehydration and hangovers. One stood out. He was tall, handsome, sandy-haired and wearing a reporter's trademark trench coat.

"The Scotsman?" I asked, extending my hand.

"Aye," he smiled, shaking hands. We walked into the terminal, chatting about the flight, the humidity and so on. But the more we talked, the more puzzled he looked.

"See here," he said eventually. "I don't want to seem rude but should I *know* you?"

"I'm Peter Rhodes from the Birmingham Post," I replied. "And you're from The Scotsman."

"Ah, no," he went on. "I *am* a Scotsman." There was a flurry of apologies, expressions of good luck and I returned to my Mac-watch. Mac was one of the last off the Boeing, crumpled, unkempt and blinking in the sunshine.

"Mac of The Scotsman?" I ventured.

"Och, aye," groaned Mac. In the few yards between door and check-in, Mac explained that he didn't realise he had a business-class seat and had simply grabbed a seat in economy. He was not, he admitted, a seasoned traveller, adding that once, in Yugoslavia, the local diet had turned his stools black. At that moment I sensed Mac, bubbling with great self-deprecating anecdotes, would be excellent company for the week. And so he was. We settled in to the Mandarin Hotel in Wanchai and, like the two professionals we were, prepared for the next day's round of interviews. And then, having worked hard for a couple of hours, we decided to slip into HK for a nightcap. But only one drink, naturally.

The phone rang in my room at 9am the next day.

"Peter!" exclaimed Ranjit Peiris, our minder from HK Government. "Where the hell are you?"

Good question. I had a vague memory of a topless bar, an awful lot of gin and a midnight snack on the street involving some unfortunate creature being produced from a large jam jar and fried to order in one of the Wanchai back streets. There may be many low-risk, late night snacks available in the Far East but crispy fried frog is not among them. I'm not even sure it was frog. But I was very ill and Mac was unwakeable and our first interview of the trip had to be called off. Ranjit was furious and rightly so.

"These are important people we have lined up for you," he said. "Make sure you are ready tomorrow, 9am sharp."

"Who are we meeting tomorrow?"

"Got a pen?"

"Of course."

Ranjit gave me the name and title of the government minister we would meet on the morrow. That night could not have been more different from the gin and frog-fest of the night before.

"Who are we seeing tomorrow?" asked Mac. I consulted my shorthand note of Ranjit's message.

"Apparently it's the Minister for Security," I explained.

So that night we ate nothing but bland rice dishes and drank only sparkling water. Chastened and clear-headed, we studied everything in our press packs about security in HK. By midnight we were experts on the subject. We could have held our own in any discussion about the defence of the border, the disposition of Gurkha regiments and the fight against drug smugglers, played out at 60 knots out on the ocean with Royal Marines leaping aboard the smugglers' boats and slashing the fuel lines with razor-sharp machetes. We read all about the eternal challenge of illegal immigration and the ruses used by desperate citizens of Red China to slip into HK, which they called "the golden hills where men eat roast pork." Some Chinese men stored up their state allocation of condoms, inflated them like balloons, stuck them under their jackets and used them as buoyancy aids to swim across to HK. Only a few days before, police had been handed a shark caught locally which was found to contain a solitary Chinese-made plimsoll. We could not have been better briefed.

Suited and booted at 9am sharp the next day, Mac and I were picked up by a limousine which whisked us up the island to the Central business area. A high-speed lift shot us up the side of a skyscraper and we were ushered into a cool, lavish office, looking down on the Star Ferries ploughing their way to and from Kowloon. The very important man Ranjit had promised was sitting behind a vast desk with his name and job description on an engraved tablet facing us. In a perfect world it would have said "Minister of Security." It did not. It said: "Minister of Securities." My bloody shorthand. Mac and I thought we were meeting a security expert. Instead, eager for his interview, was an expert on banking and investment who had been briefed to expect a pair of top-flight financial journalists from two of the UK's most influential newspapers.

I looked, panic-stricken at Mac. And Mac, for the entire duration of that interview, avoided eye-contact and spoke not a word, gazing out of the window towards China. I think he was pretending to be my driver.

Strangely, that hideously ill-starred interview did not go too badly. My opening question was: "Er, aren't there a lot of banks in Hong Kong?" which looks as pathetic on paper as it did that bright morning 22 floors up in HK. The Minister of Securities' eyes brightened.

"You know," he agreed brightly. "That's a very good question."

"Really?"

"Why, yes." And off he went, God bless him, on a long, impassioned tirade on the issue of overbanking in the territory which was, apparently, a subject close to his heart. What's more, we learned later, it was a subject some politicians and journalists chose to ignore. He admired our perception. Jackpot. Mac and I had a good interview under our belts and all that stuff about drugs, sharks and condoms would make another decent feature. We had also learned to avoid street snacks.

On an assignment like this, nothing matters except the final product. Some weeks later my Hong Kong supplement appeared in the Birmingham Post and was appreciated both in Birmingham's big Chinese community and in far-off HK. From an unpromising start, it looked authoritative and professional. But it was not as good, I have to admit, as Mac's supplement for the Scotsman which was highbrow and informative and shot through with some excellent little anecdotes. He may have been a careless airline passenger and a dangerous drinking partner but the man whose stools turned black in the Balkans could write like an angel.

The End of Empire

In 1996 I returned to Hong Kong on an Army press trip to meet our local unit, the Staffordshire Regiment, who were the penultimate British battalion to garrison the territory before the 1997 handover to China. One memory stays with me. It was an afternoon in Kowloon Tong barracks. We hacks were relaxing over coffee in the ante-room when a sergeant-major of the Staffords, clipboard in hand, appeared with two officers of the People's Liberation Army, also with clipboards. It was an astonishing, perplexing moment. Communist soldiers in the mess? What was going on? And then it fell into place. It was a process I had seen many times before as one British Army regiment handed a barracks over to another. "Two tables, oak," said the WO1. "Twelve dining chairs, oak. Two dressers, oak..." As he read from his inventory, one of the Chinese officers translated for the other who then ticked his clipboard. In a few minutes the representatives of Westminster and Beijing had agreed on the contents of the dining room from furniture to teaspoons.

We were witnessing the handover of a barracks between two nations. This little exercise, conducted with nothing more warlike than pencils and clipboards, was the end of Empire and, for all the anguish that was to come 20 years later, it was a privilege to witness it.

It was in Hong Kong that I learned to sniff in a superior sort of way at people who write "towing the line." There is no W in it. It is all about toes. Back in 1982 the border between Hong Kong and the People's Republic of China was a bronze strip across the road at the northern tip of the New Territories. There I met a border official who, during the chaos of China's Cultural Revolution in the 1960s, had been a junior officer in the British Army detachment at the border. The border itself was a flat, open area, impossible to defend. So the British garrison has retreated a few hundred yards in hills overlooking the strip in the road. On this high ground they built fire-trenches and bunkers and prepared for the five million-strong Chinese army to sweep over at any moment. It didn't happen but for a few months it was desperately tense. The situation also demanded a daily demonstration that Britain ruled every inch of Hong Kong, right up to that bronze strip and had every intention of defending every part of it. And so every morning, in best uniform and shiniest belt, this young officer was detailed to carry out an act of pure symbolism. He marched briskly along the road and down to the border and stood for a few seconds with his toes touching the frontier between the colony and China. He was toeing the line. He was making the point that beyond this strip of metal the rule of Her Britannic Majesty applied and her subjects obeyed her, not Beijing.

"And every day as I approached," he recalled with a smile. "You could hear every Kalashnikov rifle in southern China being cocked and aimed at me."

And that's why the expression is toeing, not towing, the line.

Another lesson from Hong Kong was how corruption works, as explained to us by an officer of the Royal Hong Kong Police as we returned from a patrol inside the Walled City of Kowloon, a six-acre maze of crumbling apartment blocks where some 50,000 Hong Kongers lived. It was nightmarish and it stank and, although the RHKP officers were greeted politely by the locals, everyone knew that it was the Triad gangs, not the police or government, who ruled the roost. The tiny concrete-block apartments, designed as living space, had virtually all been turned over to family businesses with plastic injection-moulding machines pumping out an endless supply of toys and trinkets stamped with the once-familiar "made in Hong Kong." It was in the connecting corridors that people cooked and slept. But for all the squalor, the residents of the Walled City were proud and ambitious people. Mum and dad may have operated a machine 12 hours a day but their daughter was probably one of those immaculately dressed, coiffed and perfectly made-up secretaries working across the water in Hong Kong's banking quarter. The Hong Kong police had been through bad times. Riddled with corruption until the 1970s, it was cleansed by the Independent Commission Against Corruption, the ICAC always pronounced as one word "Eyeseeaycee." Our guide explained how, when he was first posted to the colony as a young police inspector, he opened his drawer one day to find his pay packet, plus a brown-paper envelope stuffed with hundreds of Hong Kong dollars.

"What's this?" he asked a senior officer.

"It's your extras." explained the older man. The penny dropped. The newcomer explained that if these were corrupt payments, he wanted no part of it.

"Look, son," explained the other with a blend of kindliness and menace. "This is our bus. You can ride on it with the rest of us or you can walk behind it. But if you stand in front of it, we'll run you down."

He decided to walk behind it. As an honest officer in a bent system he was a rare bird, until Eyeseeaycee came along and cleansed the stables.

The Falklands 1988

In the late 1970s a toothy new photographer with an easy manner and a ready smile joined the Coventry Evening Telegraph. Martin was young, keen, dedicated and, surprisingly in one barely out of school, patient. The defining thing about Martin, even against a deadline, was the time and patience he took getting the shot he wanted. Today, a digital camera will rattle off 100 images in a minute and one of them will probably be fine. Back in the 80s photographers worked with mechanical Nikon SLR (single lens reflex) cameras using rolls with a maximum of 36 frames which imposed its own discipline. Rather than blast away regardless a good photographer would wait patiently for the look, the smile, the moment. Some of the older photographers spoke fondly of the venerable Speed Graphic, the press camera of so many black-and-white movies. It came with a dozen glass-plate negatives which, for the average provincial news photographer, was expected to be a day's supply.

Behind his Nikon, Martin was reliable and professional. He stayed with the Evening Telegraph for a couple of years before joining PA, the Press Association, in a career that took him around the world.

In April 1982 Argentina invaded the Falklands. A media party was put together, including national and regional newspaper reporters and photographers.

It was a conflict that delivered some astonishing dispatches and many memorable photographs. But the defining image of the Falklands was the frigate HMS Antelope exploding during a bomb-disposal operation. The stricken ship was captured for a few seconds in a fireball. And Martin Cleaver, waiting patiently as he would have waited for a baby's smile back home in Coventry, captured that moment.

He went to war as Martin Cleaver. He came home as Martin Cleaver MBE.

I missed the Falklands War. The media party was made up of news reporters, many dispatched to Portsmouth to join the ships for no better reason than they had been on duty on the day the balloon went up. But six years later I took one of the hotly-contested press places on Fire Focus '88 (Falkland Islands Reinforcement Exercise). The aim was to show the world how quickly the Falklands garrison could be reinforced and, at the pre-exercise briefing I had a stand-up row with someone from Fleet Street who couldn't see why a provincial hack should be taking a seat which rightly belonged to him. The composition of media parties on military operations and exercises is always contentious and is usually sorted out in peacetime. There is a science to it, based on getting a spread of media (newspapers, radio, television, etc) coupled with the limitations of transport in the field. There is no point, for example, in assembling a media party of twelve if the helicopter will carry only nine. I recall an MoD session in Whitehall where we media (I was speaking for the provincial press) hammered out with the military the agreed mix of media for a given party size. A fiery lady from Broadcasting House represented the BBC and she was a warrior. In her view, the ideal media party would include BBC Television, BBC Radio, BBC World Service and, of course, BBC local radio. Fleet Street's finest nodded along gallantly.

"Just a moment," I interjected. "If she gets her way, the media party in the next war will be comprised entirely of BBC TV and radio and there won't be a single seat for the written media."

They saw the point. The haggling began in earnest.

It was that sort of horse-trading which resulted in the Fire Focus 88 media pack including just one writer from Fleet Street, a couple of provincial journalists, a combined ITV/BBC television crew led by Jon Snow and, to my joy, Martin Cleaver MBE.

The RAF TriStar, rammed with squaddies and the media party, landed at Ascension Island where Jon Snow headed straight for the nearest phone (pre-mobiles, naturally) and began a heated discussion with his office. The rest of us took the view that you can have a row with the boss any time but only on Ascension Island can you buy Ascension Island T-shirts and Ascension Island mugs. We hit the island's busy little souvenir shop with a vengeance. The flight seemed endless but eventually we began the long descent into Mount Pleasant Airport. Unexpectedly, we had an escort. Two death-grey RAF Phantom fighter jets, laden with missiles and gun pods, positioned themselves off the TriStar's port and starboard wing tips. I dare say they were abiding by flight-safety rules but they seemed awfully close, too close for comfort. Scarily close. I can't recall a more frightening moment airborne. I was reminded of the Duke of Wellington's verdict on his soldiers: "I don't know what effect these men will have upon the enemy, but, by God, they frighten me."

We landed and transferred to an RAF helicopter where Cleaver chatted above the roar of the rotors with another Falklands War veteran, Ian Bruce of the Glasgow Herald. They fell silent as we flew over a slope just outside Port Stanley where the war effectively ended. As the Argentine retreat began with ones and twos running, a single RAF Harrier dropped a 1,000lb bomb on a command post on this slope. The enemy fled. The war was won. But it had been a terrible conflict and, as we swept over the scene of such carnage both men were subdued.

It was a fascinating trip. My nightly dispatches were by Telex and we were supposed to advise the army commcen of the calls we made, to pay the bill.

"Can you charge this one to the Express & Star?" I asked the duty sergeant.

"No problem," he interrupted. "So that's the Daily Express and Daily Star."

It was not the first time the E&S name had been mistaken for something in Fleet Street and, as we never got a bill for the Telex, I can only assume that Express Newspapers of London picked up my tab. Many thanks.

On the third day of the trip the party had a choice of visits and Martin Cleaver had to miss a tour of the Argentine war cemetery. He needed some stock pictures of this sad little burial ground with rows of white wooden crosses and asked if I'd take a few. He handed me a Nikon and, a few hours later, I posed an obliging British officer at the cemetery, head bowed for the doomed conscripts of the Malvinas invasion who four years earlier had the misfortune to be pitched into battle against the Royal Marines, the Paras, the Guards and the Gurkhas. I took several shots from behind the officer. At first he stood with his hands clasped in front of him. Something didn't look right. I asked him to stand as before, head bowed, but this time with his hands clasped behind him. It was only when the prints were processed that my misgivings were confirmed. The hands-behind images were excellent. It was the unmistakable image of a British officer honouring the defeated enemy. The hands-in-front photos looked like a British officer urinating on the Argentine graves. I have never believed the old adage that the camera cannot lie. It certainly can and, with a fake caption, those images could have started riots in Buenos Aires.

It was the contrast between the flower-decked British cemetery and the pitiful, wilting posies on the Argentine graves that produced some of the best articles from that media trip. My piece, Flowers for the Vanquished, and others in similar angry vein in other newspapers, led to questions in the House of Commons. The shameful logjam of delivering flowers to the islands was reviewed and streamlined. A few years later the first pilgrimage by Argentine families to the graves of their boy soldiers went ahead. Sometimes we report the news, sometimes we make the news. And sometimes we are a force for good. This is what I wrote.

FLOWERS FOR THE VANQUISHED
Port Stanley, July 1988
The story of the flowers is enough to make your heart bleed. Brook Hardcastle, general manager of the Falkland Islands Company, told it as he entertained us to lunch at his home in Darwin Settlement. Here, six years ago, high-explosive crashed and tracer flickered through the night sky as the Paras fought their way up the narrow

neck of land towards a collection of huts called Goose Green. The scars remain. Mr Hardcastle points with pride to the bullet holes where stray shots peppered his comfortable, timber-clad house on that extraordinary night. A knocked-out Argentinian gun is on display in his garden, aimed impotently at the sapphire-blue creek where he caught our lunch, a 12lb sea trout, a couple of days ago.

Not far away is the Argentinian war cemetery where the glare from 250 white wooden crosses hurts your eyes as the sun blasts down from a deep azure sky. Some have names. But most of Galtieri's half-trained conscripts were not even given identity tags and their graves carry the motto: "An Argentinian Soldier Known Unto God." Most of the British bodies have been brought home. Today, just twenty-five remain in the neat military cemetery at Port San Carlos, overlooking the landing beaches of 'Bomb Alley' where enemy pilots showed such courage. But there is no going home for the Argentinians, not as long as Buenos Aires refuses even to discuss the matter for fear of acknowledging British sovereignty.

Meanwhile, the unending saga of claim and counter-claim to these islands turns even the simplest gesture by heartbroken Argentinian families into a bureaucratic morass. To send flowers to the graves of Los Chicos de la Guerra (The Children of the War), relatives must first pass them to the Brazilian embassy in Buenos Aires. The pathetic little parcels are then flown 7,000 miles to Britain, handed over to our Foreign Office, put in the diplomatic bag and flown 8,000 miles back to the Falklands. The Governor, Gordon Jewkes, dispatches them by helicopter to Mr Hardcastle who in turn takes them to the cemetery. The tiny bouquets never have names, he says. Just messages in Spanish like 'My Beloved' or 'My Little Dove'. So he places them by whichever of the crosses catches his eye.

Walk northwards from Brook Hardcastle's home over the springy, gale-bent heather and you come to a small valley leading from the seashore towards the high ground.

On the left of this valley is a cairn of white stones; on the right, about a hundred yards away, a timber peg driven into the thin earth. Here, Lieutenant-Colonel 'H' Jones, furious and frustrated that the left flank of his assault was bogged down, launched his desperately brave one-man attack. The timber peg marks the trench from which the fatal burst of machine-gunfire came. The cairn shows where Jones fell. The colonel's grave is at Port San Carlos, a sprig of pink blossom brushing against the VC carved into the headstone. There are a dozen wreaths at the gates, plants on every grave.

For the victors, there is no shortage of flowers from family, comrades and islanders. For the vanquished, unknown in these distant graves, come occasional posies, wilting from the idiotic, unforgivable, 15,000-mile flight that pride and politics demand.

In the years that followed, newspapers both national and regional marked the anniversaries of the 1982 Falklands conflict, meeting and interviewing the veterans and recording their memories. Many of these eyewitness testimonies never made it into the national media but provide a priceless insight into that war and the men who contested it. The Falklands was unlike the two world wars in that it involved a generation which had not been raised to know its place and hold its peace. These were professional soldiers, sailors and aircrew. I never met one who didn't think the Falklands War could and should have been averted by diplomacy. But I also never met one who was not proud to have been there. Men like Terry Bullingham, blinded on HMS Antrim:

The last thing Terry Bullingham ever saw was two Argentinian Mirage jets, head-on.

'It was like an air show,' he recalls at his Smethwick home. 'They were so low and going too fast to register properly. Then there was a sound like calico ripping, only many times louder.'

It was the roar of the warplanes opening fire with their cannon. Shells exploded around the flight deck of the Royal Navy destroyer HMS Antrim.

Chief Petty Officer Bullingham felt 'a sickening blow' and, at the age of thirty-seven, his world went black. It was May 21, 1982. HMS Antrim, providing air defence for the troopship Canberra, had been struck by two Argentinian bombs which failed to explode. Next came a strafing attack which left a cluster of crew injured and CPO Bullingham blinded.

'We heard this huge metallic ring as the bomb struck. We didn't know whether it had gone off or not. We were busy cooling the decks with water. Then we saw the Mirages. I was hit in the arms and leg. I remember going into the foetal position. Someone said, "You've got a couple of black eyes" and I thought, he's lying.'

Terry Bullingham is relentlessly upbeat. If you have to be blinded, he says, it's far better to lose it instantly.

'It just went black. No shades of grey. No flashes of light. No anxiety. Nothing to distract your brain. Just total blackness and two plastic eyes. Now you see it, now you don't.'

Or Steve McIntosh, a teenager who witnessed the most controversial moment of the war, the sinking of the Argentine cruiser, General Belgrano:

They had trained, trained and trained again. In May 1982, the crew of Her Majesty's Submarine Conqueror were part of a silent, elite force. They were deep in the South Atlantic, tracking a warship whose name was soon to pass into history.

'None of us had been to war before,' says Steve McIntosh from Bilston, 'It was just like another exercise when we went to action stations.'

The submarine had been tracking the Argentinian cruiser General Belgrano for days. On board Conqueror, Steve was a seventeen-year-old contact evaluation plotter in the control room.

'All the information was getting relayed back to the Government in London. We did ask permission to engage her and we were knocked back several times.'

Finally, Whitehall authorised Belgrano's destruction.

'We were carrying wire-guided torpedoes but we decided to use Mk 8s, the World War Two torpedo, fired in salvoes of three. We could hear everything. We could feel the submarine shake slightly as they were fired. We could hear them running for a while and then everything went silent. Then we heard two impacts. It was like a thud and a hollow clap, and a weird tinkling. That was the metal of the ship breaking up. There was also the smell of cordite coming back up the torpedo tubes.

'At first, the mood was fantastic. But when it sank in we thought, what have we done? Although we were at war, it wasn't as though we thought about the enemy as people. The Belgrano was a big and very, very dangerous ship. We knew we had to disarm it, to make sure there was no confrontation with the Task Force.'

After the attack on the Belgrano the British submarine went 'fast and deep' to avoid the cruiser's smaller escort ships.

'Later on there was a service on board. We prayed for those who had been left behind by their escorts.'

Does he have any regrets about sinking the Belgrano?

'I was very young and I didn't push the button. We were all part of a team. We trained all the time. On the sub, it was very clear. I thought it was a shame that people lost their lives but I still think it was either them or us. I felt sorry for their sailors because they were conscripts. No way were they as good as we were.'

Or Dean Jenkins, a 19-year-old Para who witnessed the death of Colonel 'H' Jones in the attack at Goose Green: 'There was this sniper. He must have killed three of our lads. Every time anyone climbed over the fence, he fired. It reminded me of the First World War and going over the top.'

The attack faltered. The paras were pinned down in a shallow gully. It was then that their furious colonel arrived. 'Everyone recognised H Jones. He was tall, wearing this padded jacket and he was shouting and moaning that we had all stopped. We were a bit aggrieved. We'd been under fire for two hours and here we were, getting the blame.'

At that moment H Jones launched his one-man attack on an Argentinian trench. As he reached it, he was killed by a burst of machine-gun fire from another trench. The debate on whether he was a hero or a fool has raged ever since. What no-one denies is that the paras, robbed of their CO, fought like demons.

'Someone used an anti-tank rocket to destroy an enemy bunker. The Argentinians didn't seem to know what to do next. We went into our trench-clearing drill using phosphorous grenades. We literally overran them. We ran out of grenades. My partner covered me and I got to the edge of a trench. These two Argentinians were coming out...'

He speaks quietly with not a profane word. There is no swagger, no remorse as this former Para and policeman recalls the deed.

'I didn't think about killing at the time but afterwards we were all in this state of shock, tired and amazed that we should have survived. I can see us now after the battle, all white-eyed and white-lipped.'

At last, we have buried the Cold War

The 20th century was a century of wars. The one that threatened to wipe out humanity is the one, strangely enough, that slipped almost instantly into history. Today's kids have hardly heard of it. But from 1945 until 1989 the Cold War dictated everything.

In 1983, on a press trip to Berlin with the British Army, I stood on the roof of the Reichstag, an army observation post, and looked down on this divided city, divided Germany, divided world. The Berlin Wall and the Inner German Frontier were stamped across the land in steel and concrete. If there was one certainty in 1983 it was that these barriers, like Hadrian's Wall, would last for centuries.

And then six years later it was all over. The world changed and the Wall came down. Within a few weeks it was announced that President Bush (the older) of the USA and President Mikhail Gorbachev of Russia would meet in Malta at a special conference to sign the agreements that would bring the Cold War to an end.

"We ought to be there," said the E&S deputy editor Derek Tucker about two weeks before the conference. By which, of course, he meant you ought to be there. And someone should have made the decision ages ago. From time to time you will meet journalists who claim to be in charge of forward planning at their newspaper. Do not believe a word of it. Most newsrooms look no further forward than the next day's paper or the next week's supplement. The idea of starting a project weeks, or ideally months, in advance is alien to the beast. I lost count of the number of times some breathless reporter on Newsdesk would phone Features with something on these lines:

"Oh, hi. We're going to do a supplement next week to mark the centenary of the City Theatre."

"Really. And what's the deadline?"

"We'd like the interviews, photos and artwork from you by next Monday."

"So that's three days. And how much warning did we have of this centenary?"

"How do you mean?"

"Well, would I be right in thinking that we have known this anniversary was coming for about, say, a hundred years?"

"Oh, I see. Sorry."

And the job would be done at silly speed with none of the interviews that could have been fixed with a little more notice. And the supplement would look okay but nothing more than okay. And everyone would agree that what the paper really needed was someone in charge of forward planning. But not just yet.

With the Malta summit just a few days away I booked accommodation. All the hotels in the capital Valletta were jammed and I had to settle for the only one-star hotel in the Thomson catalogue out on the road to Sliema. And because Malta was a sunny place, even in December, my wife came too. And so did our three-year-old daughter who was just developing a worrying sniffle. And my mother in law. And just about everything that could go wrong went wrong.

We set off for Manchester Airport in thick fog. The drive was atrocious. As we got to the airport, all the baggage handlers walked out on strike. We were put on a coach for Luton Airport. Thus, 12 hours after passing Junction 4 on the M6 northbound, we passed it southbound. Luton Airport was terrific; from entering the terminal to taking off took just 20 minutes. In the early hours of Day One of the summit we landed in Malta where the rain was coming down in sheets and our little girl was not only sniffling but running a temperature. I had no accreditation for the summit, no story to file and the Tandy laptop refused to make a connection on its dedicated phone line to Wolverhampton.

The misery worsened the next day. At the conference centre we learned that there would be no interviews with anybody who mattered. Bush, Gorbachev and their aides, including big players like the Kremlin spokesman Gennadi Gerasimov, were meeting on a warship three miles out at sea. The media plan was that each day 12 hacks would be selected from the 2,500 attending and flown to the ship where they would be given a briefing. All 12 would then write their dispatches which would be made available to all of us. There was the horrible moment all journalists experience at some stage when you realise there is absolutely nothing you can do 1,000 miles from home that you couldn't do just as well, or better, from home.

Even the famed walkabout by Gorbachev's elegant wife was not guaranteed. An Italian reporter with barely enough English to order breakfast, plaintively asked the press officer time after time: "Raisa, she is walk, she is no walk?"

I slumped back into the hotel where the doctor had been called. He diagnosed our daughter with scarlet fever. She was sick and feverish and ghostly white but in good spirits. It was a family hotel in the best sense and everyone wanted to know about the beautiful little English girl who was poorly. Our baby was a star. At one stage, she appeared on the landing and a Maltese maid fell to her knees, clasped her hands in adoration and exclaimed: "Oh, oh! She is angel!"

It was a cheap hotel which probably explained why, of the 41 reporters staying there, the other 40 were Russians. Entirely by chance, late booking and cheapness, I found myself in the Russian media centre.

At this stage I was convinced this was a wasted mission. There was no hope of getting anything original, let alone that jewel-encrusted Holy Grail we call a scoop.

On the final day of the "Salt Water Summit" I returned to the hotel where a Russian reporter was just finishing a furtive conversation with the receptionist.

"Anything happening?" I inquired. And because of our poorly little girl and the bond it had created with the staff, the receptionist chatted freely.

"There is someone important here," she whispered.

"Do you know his name?"

"Gerasimov?" she ventured.

"What? Do you mean Gennadi Gerasimov?"

"Yes. That's him in the bar," she said pointing to the half-open door.

I went in and took a bar stool. Gerasimov, a big figure wrapped in a fur coat, took the next stool. I showed him my press pass. He nodded. And in that sweetest of sweet moments I had my scoop. For at the very moment the Cold War ended and the world found a moment of joy and radiant hope, the Kremlin's best-known spokesman was talking one-to-one not to the New York Times or the Washington Post, nor to Le Monde or the Times of London or BBC World Service. Gennadi Gerasimov was talking to the Express & Star from Wolverhampton. And this, beginning with a half-remembered line from Casablanca, is the dispatch:

The Bush/Gorbachev Summit, Malta. December 1989

Of all the bars in all the gin joints in all the world, Gennadi Gerasimov had to walk into mine. The head of information at the Kremlin, anxious to escape the crush of two thousand foreign journalists in the centre of Valletta last night, booked into the cheapest room in the down-market Sa Maison Hotel on the road to Sliema and pulled up the bar stool next to mine. There are forty-one journalists staying at this hotel. The other forty are

88

Russians. As the sole representative of the free world's media, I presented my credentials to the great man as he thoughtfully cradled a half of lager.

'Wolverhampton...?'

Near Birmingham, I explained.

'Ah, Birmingham. I was there once a long time ago.' Brum did not seem to have left much of an impression.

His verdict on the Malta Summit?

'Very good. At last we have buried the Cold War, deep in the deepest part of the Mediterranean. Right at the bottom of the sea where it will stay from here to eternity.'

His hopes for the June Summit, announced yesterday?

'By the time of the Summit, START (the Strategic Arms Reduction Talks), must be finished. We want to have a real Summit and that is a realistic possibility if the political will is there. Malta was a meeting of minds. It was brain-storming on what to do next in this awful world of ours. Next June we will actually sign important documents concerning nuclear and conventional weapons. Then the British official position, in support of nuclear weapons, will look outdated. These weapons have nothing to do with keeping the peace. They are just your expensive toys to play with and some toys are dangerous. They can spoil the whole Midlands.' He grinned.

'The bigger the cuts in arms and men next June, the better. What are British troops doing in Germany? What are Soviet troops doing in Germany? They must go away, all of them. What are British troops doing in the Rhineland – why are they not in your Midlands...?'

The quote I lifted from Casablanca could have been more accurate. What Bogart actually says in the film is: "Of all the gin joints, in all the towns, in all the world, she walks into mine."

Today, it takes a few minutes on the internet to get it word-perfect. Back in the 1980s you'd need a dictionary of notable film quotes from your local library. As a reporter in those days you relied on the facts you carried in your head, coupled with the knowledge that, even if a reader thought you'd got the quote wrong, it would take him ages to find out for sure.

And so the Cold War slipped into history and out of memory. Generations have grown up knowing nothing about the Hungarian Uprising, the Czech Spring or East Germany machine-gunning its civilians who tried to flee. How many of today's under-40s, for example, have heard of Chapman Pincher? He was the ultimate spy-unmasking journalist during the Cold War. I interviewed him once at length on the publication of his book Traitors and had a few conversations with him in later life (he died in 2014, aged 100). Nothing depressed him more than the unseemly haste with which past treachery was forgiven. His business had been exposing traitors among MPs and in the heart of Britain's security service. But as Russia became our friend – albeit briefly – who cared about past betrayals? One day in 2011 we were chatting by email when I said people no longer seemed interested in the spies and subversives of the Cold War. "I get the message," Chapman Pincher wrote tersely. I never heard from him again.

Scoop!

The Gerasimov interview fulfilled all the requirements of a classic newspaper scoop. Not only had I managed to get a face-to-face interview with no other media present and an exclusive story but, thanks to evening-newspaper deadlines, it would be fully 24 hours before rival daily newspapers could do what we all call "the follow-up" which actually means "nicking it." As a feature writer, you don't expect to get many scoops; that's the territory of the 'ard-nosed 'acks who call themselves "investigative reporters" (which poses the question: what sort of reporter is not investigative?). But from time to time, even in Sleepy Hollow, scoops come along.

When the Falklands War of 1982 suddenly turned serious the Government announced the sinking of the warships HMS Sheffield and HMS Coventry, the first by an Exocet missile, the second by old-fashioned, and possibly British-made, bombs. As the bad news kept coming, the nation was horrified. The admiral's famous outburst at the Battle of Jutland in 1916 suddenly rang true again: "Something wrong with our bloody ships today." Eight thousand miles from the Falklands, in the newsroom of the Birmingham Post & Mail, I was working a night shift when someone handed me a slip of paper with a name and phone number. "Give this bloke a ring," he said. "He might have something to say."

Captain John Moore RN was editor of Jane's Fighting Ships. We had never spoken before and the phone interview began with some general questions about naval warfare and the threat to the British Task Force. Then I asked the obvious question. What was wrong with our bloody ships? Why were the Argies able to sink them so easily? There was a pause as Moore gathered his thoughts, a moment of hesitation. Journalists come to recognise this moment and cherish it, for it is the instant when somebody makes the decision to tell you something significant.

"Well, I suppose there's no harm in saying it now," said John Moore. And he told of a long, bitter argument between old-style sailors like himself, who recalled the days when a British frigate could survive a 1,000-lb bomb strike and still sail home, and a modern generation of man-managers desperate to find recruits in post National Service times when every fresh-faced matelot was a volunteer.

In order to attract recruits, ships had been made more user-friendly. Steel hatches had been replaced with aluminium doors, hard benches replaced with soft foam cushions. And, because young men love their chips and expect a daily fry-up, the kitchens on front-line warships carried gallons of cooking oil. The destroyers and frigates of the 1980s were infinitely more comfortable than those of the 1940s but, as we were learning in the Falklands, they burned and sank.

"Some of us have been making this argument for years," said Moore, resignedly.

So there was something wrong with our bloody ships, after all. And it was a provincial newspaper in land-locked Birmingham that gave the answer. A little scoop but a scoop for all that.

Jack Straw provided another little scoop and a memorable day for an unhappy police officer. It was during the General Election campaign of 1997 and Straw, soon to become Home Secretary in Tony Blair's government, was on a tour of Labour marginals in the Midlands and had agreed to stop at the Express & Star offices in Wolverhampton for a 30-minute interview. As things turned out, Straw was with us for much longer. For that was the day the IRA claimed to have planted a bomb beside the M6. The area was locked down and surrounding roads jam-packed. The Shadow Home Secretary was going nowhere for four hours. So he stayed for tea and sandwiches and we gave him a tour of the offices and press hall and the planned half-hour interview turned into a long, informal chat about this, that and everything, including the obvious question: wouldn't he prefer to be standing as Labour leader rather than Tony Blair?

"Not at all," smiled Straw. "Tony's a star."

At the time, he seemed to be not entirely serious, parroting the party script. With hindsight I suspect he was absolutely serious. Blair didn't work his magic on everybody but he had an extraordinary ability to connect with people and win General Elections. The conversation turned to the IRA and Straw mentioned in passing that, as a junior barrister, he had been wounded by the IRA bomb at the Old Bailey in 1973.

"Really?" I replied. "I've never read that anywhere."

"No," said Straw. "I don't think I've ever mentioned it in public."

"And where were you wounded?"

"Mm. It's not exactly a scar you can show off," said Straw. "It was a small piece of glass, in the backside."

Again, not the biggest scoop in the world but it does show how leaving your prepared list of questions behind and chatting informally can reveal some strange things. As far as I am aware, the Express & Star was the only newspaper to report after Blair's triumphant landslide, that Mr Straw who would be dealing with the IRA, had the unique distinction among Home Secretaries of being wounded by an IRA bomb. We did not go into the grisly details.

As the IRA M6 incident turned out to be a hoax, Jack Straw prepared to leave the E&S office and thanked us for our hospitality.

"Look, Peter," he said as we shook hands, "in a few weeks I might be Home Secretary. If you ever need any help with anything, just give me a call."

I thought no more about it. A few weeks later we had a particularly savage mugging in Wolverhampton. It was unusual for three reasons. Firstly, the 80-year-old victim was a former hairdresser and well known in the city. Secondly, she was a police officer's widow. Thirdly, this was the seventh time she had been mugged and none of the attackers had been caught. She was a pitiful sight, her old face blackened with bruises. She was a hairdresser and I needed a haircut. So I took a seat and, as she cut my hair, we talked. She was a lovely, gentle lady with the misfortune to have settled years ago in a once-genteel and cherished part of Wolverhampton which had sunk over the years into a morass of drug-dealing and street crime. She was resigned to yobbery in the street outside and did not expect the police to capture the thug who battered her on her own doorstep and stole her handbag.

Back at the office, writing the feature in rising anger and indignation, I suddenly thought, why the hell not? I called my new best friend, the Home Secretary. Jack Straw was unavailable but an aide seemed genuinely interested in the case and took a full note. I heard nothing back from Straw but, a couple of hours later my phone rang. The caller was possibly the angriest and most frightened copper I have ever encountered.

He had been enjoying a quiet morning at the nick when his phone rang and he found himself being harangued by the Home Secretary. Straw explained, in robust terms, that he was not happy with the police handling of this mugging and he wanted results. The officer was in a foul mood. The Home Office had given him all the details of the case, except the woman's name. He demanded to know her identity and his mood worsened when I said I'd have to check with her first but, in any case, how many police widows who had been mugged seven times did he have on his patch?

Later we heard that the police had interviewed the old lady. And soon after that they got their man. I was pleased with the outcome and reflected on the value of contacts in high place. A few weeks later Jack Straw, by now Home Secretary and still my bestest best friend in Whitehall, came to Wolverhampton to declare a new police station officially open. In the brief press conference that followed, I caught Straw's eye and smiled.

"Sorry," said the Home Secretary, "have we met before…?"

And then there are the scoops you miss…

Sometimes you miss them despite them being offered to you on a silver platter with a side order of celebrity. At the end of 1981 when I was on the Birmingham Post & Mail, the BBC announced it would soon be screening an adaptation of Fame is the Spur, a series based on the novel by Howard Spring. It's about a socialist politician who betrays his early beliefs as he grows older; some believe it was based on the Labour Prime Minister Ramsay MacDonald. And it triggered something profound and principled in the heartstrings of the Features Editor, Clem Lewis. He was an old-fashioned socialist, a good, caring man whose beliefs had been founded on literature like this. He believed the Great British Public would be bowled over by this TV series (in the event, they were not) and he wanted a big, full-page feature about it. I was dispatched to a grim rehearsal room in London where one of the young stars of Fame is the Spur, Tim Pigott-Smith was delighted to talk about the series, the book and its message for people of today. I liked Pigott-Smith. He was the son of the editor of the Stratford-upon-Avon Herald which qualified him, for Post & Mail purposes as "a Midland actor." But what he really wanted to talk about was this amazing epic he had been filming in India.

He was clearly astonished by the sale of the production, the heat, the dust of India and the glittering, globally-known actors he was working with. However, my brief from the old socialist features editor in Birmingham was a feature about Fame is the Spur. And that's what I produced. Tim Pigott-Smith tried to drag me off-message with his epic tale of the Raj but I refused to be dragged. And that is how I came to write a feature about an old book which I doubt was of interest to more than a few hundred of the Evening Mail's 250,000 readers. In the process I entirely ignored the Indian thing. A couple of years later Granada screened The Jewel in the Crown, one of the finest and most-watched costume dramas in television history, starring Tim Pigott-Smith as the villainous cop, Ronald Merrick. So that's what he'd been talking about. Thanks to him, I'd been given more than enough information to do a whole series of features on The Jewel in the Crown, months before the rest of the press pack, and ignored it.

"Look at this," said Clem Lewis as the Jewel in the Crown press pack arrived from Granada. "It's starring Tim Pigott-Smith. Didn't you interview him for us...?"

1990 Hello, Moscow – welcome to capitalism

The next year, 1990, was hectic. In the summer I was sent to Moscow after the E&S Editor Keith Parker declared in morning conference: "Looks like civil war in Russia – get Rhodes out there!" Parker loved saying things like that. He was a great editor and a great believer in the "total newspaper." In his book it was not enough for a regional newspaper to carry only regional or local news. Unless it offered a full and independent package of national and international news, people on our patch would choose a national newspaper instead. His "total newspaper" philosophy explained why, in the 1980s, the Express & Star was reaching almost a million readers every day and was read in 70 per cent of the homes across our circulation area.

It also explains why an editor based in Wolverhampton wanted his journalists competing with the national press pack, wherever it took them. Thus, in 1979 he dispatched Tony Bishop to the North-West Frontier to report on the Soviet invasion of Afghanistan. The rumour in the E&S was that Parker asked: "Which of our district offices is nearest to Kabul?"

"Stourbridge," replied a reporter.

"And who's the chief reporter at Stourbridge?"

"Tony Bishop."

"Then get Bishop out there."

Bishop did a fine job, even if the arrival of the provincial press at the front took some Fleet Street hands by surprise. "The Wolverhampton Express & Star?" exclaimed Robert Fisk of The Times. "They'll be sending Exchange & Mart next."

I flew to Moscow early in 1990 by the simple process of booking on a Thomas Cook package trip and lying about my job on the visa form. With hindsight, I'm not even sure that the word "journalist," which slammed so many doors in authoritarian states (I never did get to Albania), would have been a problem. For this was a Russia transformed from what I had seen in Leningrad 14 years earlier. Back then, the streets were unremittingly gloomy and the store windows unlit. In a state-run economy there was no need to advertise, no need to hang out any lights. Moscow, 1990, was another world, the Wild West of the East. The dodgy money-changers who once skulked just out of sight, were plying their illicit trade in full view. The stores blazed with light, there were Coca-Cola stands and around the new McDonald's off Gorki Square the queue was long and excited. "For us," explained one English-speaking Muscovite, with a view that would once have sent him straight to the gulags, "this is like a day in the West."

The threatened civil war had not erupted but the social collapse surrounding the end of the USSR was everywhere. In a subway by Red Square the man hustling to sell cheap Russian watches was a doctor. He made more money selling watches for a week than being a doctor for a month. He wanted 10 dollars. I gave him 20. "You shame me, you shame me!" he exclaimed, close to tears. Not at all, I explained.

"I'm a journalist," I told him. "You give me information. I pay for information. No shame. Welcome to capitalism."

Off to war in the Gulf

In the summer of 1990 Saddam Hussein, president of Iraq, invaded Kuwait and declared that, as Province 19, it was part of Iraq. The rest of the world disagreed. A huge coalition under UN rules was formed and a mighty land and air armada was assembled in the borders of Iraq and Kuwait.

For me, the first Gulf War began in September 1990 when, as a Territorial Army officer, I was on exercise on the vast Sennelager training area in Germany. The phone in our media centre rang. It was the Commanding Officer of the British Army's media-operations pool.

"Peter," he said. "Can you come out here?"

"Out where?"

"To the Gulf. I'm in Riyadh."

"You mean we're being mobilised?"

"Not exactly. You'll have to come as a volunteer for three months. Can you get the time off work?"

"Of course I can't, Colonel. What I need from you is the piece of paper to show my employer and my wife that I am being called up and have no choice in this."

"Entirely understand," said the colonel. "But you know how I am – first whiff of gunpowder and I've got to be there. So if you possibly could…"

Back at the office in Wolverhampton I explained the dilemma to the Editor. As soon as I was mobilised I would willingly do my bit. But I had no intention of going anywhere in uniform without being formally mobilised, with all the pay, pension and other security that involves. I said it would help my case greatly if my employer refused to release me, if he were to say something on the lines of "I want you here."

"I want you here," said Keith Parker. A great editor.

A few days later I wrote a leader-page column in the form of an open letter to the Defence Secretary Tom King, pointing out that we Territorials were ready to serve but only if he fulfilled his part of the bargain. My piece was headlined "Shabby Call to our Weekend Warriors" and ended: "If you want us, mobilise us." I heard later that King was stung by this column and ordered that this turbulent major in Wolverhampton be formally rebuked. I took comfort from a number of TA officers and soldiers who made contact to voice their appreciation and offer support.

It sparked a little victory. The MoD set about re-writing its TA mobilisation process. As the year turned, I was mobilised and, as I usually choose to put it, "I served for the duration of the land war." The land war, as any historian will tell you, lasted for about four days.

Oddly enough, some weeks before I joined the First Gulf War as a soldier I had been to the war as a journalist.

A media trip to the RAF base in Bahrain was arranged just before Christmas and I got the seat reserved for the provincial press. My description of training at Brize Norton for chemical warfare won the Feature Writer of the Year award in the Press Gazette awards. This is it:

GULF ALCHEMY AND THE SCENT OF WAR
Bahrain, December 1990

Armageddon smells of burnt almonds. At the first whiff, you must inject yourself with your Combo-pen. The Combo-pen, gentlemen. In the cold and echoing departure lounge at RAF Brize Norton the flight-sergeant held the six-inch long automatic syringe for our inspection. We watched, fascinated like the raw, astonished ranks of Kitchener's innocents, seventy-five years before. And, just like the boys in the poem, we had Naming of Parts. The Combo-pen. The S-10 respirator. The DKP decontamination paper and puffer pack. The rubber outer gloves ('just like Marigolds,' said the sergeant), the white cotton inner gloves, looking incongruously like a conjuror's gloves, to absorb the sweat.

Today, we try to remember it all, for today we are in Bahrain with the RAF strike-aircraft squadrons and well within range of the only Iraqi weapon that any of the soldiers, sailors and airmen here seem to worry about. Somewhere out there, beyond the shimmering desert horizon in the place that Saddam Hussein calls Province Nineteen and the rest of us call Kuwait, hundreds of Soviet-built Scud missiles are pointing our way.

There is nothing very sophisticated about Scud. It is as primitive as its name sounds, a big rocket which is simply pointed at the infidel, launched at the appropriate elevation and lobbed in a ballistic arc. Because it is so simple, because it contains no hi-tech guidance, there is no micro-chip means of sending it off course. The Allied half of the Gulf is dotted with American batteries of Patriot missiles which, on exercises, regularly knock out more than ninety per cent of Scud-type targets. It is surprising how worrying ten per cent can be. Scud can carry explosives, but in the British force area no-one is ever far from a bomb-proof shelter. The real nightmare is Scud's alternative payload, nerve gas, which arrives with no more warning than a few blue dots on the detector paper of your NBC suit or the faintest hint of burnt almonds.

What was it the sergeant told us? Turn your back to the bombardment, tuck your head close to your respirator bag and pull on the face mask. Blow out hard, shouting gas, gas, gas!

And wait. And hope that none of the following symptoms begins: breathlessness, sweating, uncontrolled movements, involuntary urination or defecation. If that happens, break the seal of your Combo-pen, hold it against the fleshy part of your thigh and press the trigger. The sergeant demonstrated on a beret, the wicked inch-long needle flashing into the fabric, spitting a fine spray of atropine, a dose which, with luck, might counteract the nerve agent as it seeps into your system breaking down the muscle functions that keep your heart pumping, your lungs working.

Just as Scud is primitive, so the counter-measures seem to owe more to medieval alchemy than the twentieth century. Atropine to strengthen your heartbeat. Belladonna tablets to reduce panic. Fuller's earth to absorb the nerve-gas droplets. You look at the Combo-pen, you feel the clumsiness of your hands in two pairs of gloves. You suddenly understand what the war poet Wilfred Owen was talking about in Dulce et Decorum Est, his harrowing poem of a soldier drowning in chlorine because he was too slow with his gas mask. You understand 'an ecstasy of fumbling'.

A corporal donned the full 'noddy suit' to demonstrate how to drink water when the air is thick with nerve gas. From the front of his respirator he uncoiled a rubber tube and clipped it into his drinking bottle. As he held the bottle high and drank it looked like *some nightmarish bug-eyed moth, sipping nectar through its coiled proboscis. When the sergeant finished his hour-long briefing, part of our media party burst into spontaneous applause. They were not news hacks like the rest of us but a posse of quiet, rather thoughtful technicians and cameramen from the BBC over here to record Songs of Praise from the Gulf on Christmas Eve. It will be an incongruous event, a brief link between the real Britain of mortgages and foggy mornings and this other England in a sunny, sandy corner of the world where your sleeping companion is your S-10 respirator and your best pal is your Combo-pen.*

Today I visited a Rapier anti-aircraft position and bumped into Corporal Simon 'Spike' Horton, from Low Hill, Wolverhampton, who has spent his time-off from manning the battery in making a snowman out of chicken wire and toilet paper and finding wall space in his cramped billet for a couple of paintings from his three-year-old nephew Garth. This gift, he confesses, moved him more than he had expected. But the mood here is neither maudlin nor fearful. It is busy, purposeful and confident. It's just that now and then a child's painting may move a soldier to tears or thoughts of Scud and the idea of almonds on the breeze make you check you Combo-pens for the twentieth time and wish you had paid more attention to what goes on back home in your own kitchen.

There are nine of us on this media trip, all male, and none of us thought to ask the most obvious question of all back at Brize Norton. It is a little worrying that, come Armageddon, none of us has the faintest idea what burnt almonds smell like.

Out in Bahrain, there was a brief interview with the RAF's oldest combat pilot in the Gulf, Squadron Leader Dave 'Baggers' Bagshaw who was 53 and a grandfather of four. He had served at the same air base, then RAF Muharraq, during the 1967 Aden crisis. He showed us some Christmas cards sent to his Jaguar squadron by children near their base back in East Anglia. One read: "Dear Dads and Men in the Gulf, we hope you don't get shot for Christmas."

The most moving encounter, but only with hindsight, was one I couldn't find space for in my dispatches. On the final day of the media trip to Bahrain, the BBC hosted a dinner for the hacks and the RAF Tornado crews. The pilots and navigators were upbeat. They knew their job was perilous and their Tornados dated, but took comfort from being part of a massive air armada, led by the United States. In particular, they admired the performance, ruggedness and survivability of the Americans' F-15 bombers. As dinner ended we had what I can only describe as a 1940 moment. In that year, with things going badly in the Battle of Britain, the Luftwaffe commander Hermann Goering berated his squadron commanders in northern France and demanded to know if there was anything they needed to drive the RAF from the skies.

The air ace Adolf Galland famously replied: "A squadron of Spitfires."

As our dinner ended in Bahrain, the BBC man made a short speech wishing the RAF men well and asked if there was anything they needed, something that the folks back home could supply. The answer came in a split-second.

"F-15s" they chorused as one.

Next job: war criminal

A few weeks later I was formally mobilised for the Gulf War as Major Rhodes, Royal Signals, and reported to HQ UK Land Forces at Wilton near Salisbury. Curiously, there was no formal induction, no issue of NBC or tropical kit, and no 9mm Browning pistol, my personal weapon. There comes a moment when every reservist discovers what his war role is. I had assumed I would be a minder, looking after one or two war correspondents in the battle zone. Far from it. On my first day at Wilton I discovered that while my civilian job was writing features for the Express & Star, my war role was writing features for Soldier magazine and the national newspapers, first in the UK and later, if required, in the Gulf.

It was a cushy number. We lived in the Royal Artillery mess at Larkhill, dined well and worked sensible hours, putting together features on the UK end of the Gulf War, including a fascinating account of how many tons of kit were being shipped daily from Marchwood Military Port near Southampton.

But the highlight of the tour of duty was at the temporary prisoner-of-war compound set up at one of the old army training camps on Salisbury Plain. As soon as Saddam Hussein invaded Kuwait the previous summer, a few dozen Iraqi students, including military reservists, were rounded up from various universities and interned on the Plain for the duration. For the Cheshire Regiment administering the camp, it was a novel experience. The British Army hadn't run a PoW camp for decades. The rules and regulations were laid down in some dusty old books from the 1940s and the Cheshires were left to calculate arcane issues such as daily allowance rates, allowing for half-a-century of inflation and the change to decimal currency. The army photographer produced some excellent images from the PoW camp (no names, no faces, obviously) and we submitted the feature to the MoD. It was rejected on the grounds that it might be held to expose the prisoners-of-war to ridicule or contempt and might therefore be a breach of the Geneva Conventions. We argued our case hard, pointing out that no-one was identified and there was no chance of derision. But the powers-that-be were unshifting and a fascinating anecdote of the war was spiked.

So here's the irony. As a journalist I went to the Gulf War, got special training and brand-new equipment and covered myself in glory at the press awards. As an army officer I went to the Gulf War, got no special training, no new equipment, never got south of Marchwood and ended up as a war criminal. Vive la difference, as they hardly ever say in Baghdad.

Working in Army public relations (or psychological operations – "psyops" – as it is now grandly styled) introduced me to one of the great truths about the media. The sheer firepower of television is astonishing. In the written media you can spend a lifetime spinning the most enchanting features or the most brilliantly penetrative political columns and you might get the occasional appreciative letter from a reader or an invitation to speak at your local Rotary Club. But if you happen to do a two-minute television interview your phone never stops ringing with excited friends, family, readers and even colleagues, who should know better, gushing excitedly: "Saw you on the telly last night!" Ah yes, you may chide them, but did you ever read my hard-hitting series on drugs in the inner-city? Of course they didn't. It was a colonel in the Army public-information unit who put the disparity between printed page and TV screen perfectly as he explained how and why we invited the various media to cover military exercises, and how nothing succeeded quite like a spot on TV news. "You see, Peter," he explained patiently. "For the written media such as newspapers and magazines, we organise media facilities. But for television, we swing by our balls from the chandelier."

The First Hercules into Sarajevo

At the end of June 1992 the Ministry of Defence put out a press release announcing that in the next few days an RAF Hercules would attempt to deliver a cargo of medical and food supplies to Sarajevo. The background to this was the break-up of Yugoslavia and civil war. Sarajevo, the mainly Muslim capital of Bosnia, was surrounded by Bosnian Serb soldiers and irregulars in a siege which, by the time it ended, would claim 10,000 innocent lives in the city. The UN declared that supplies would get through to Sarajevo and a battalion of Canadian troops duly secured the airport. But an airport is nothing unless aircraft can use it. The job of breaking the siege was given to Britain. It developed into Operation Cheshire, the longest air-supply mission in the history of the RAF.

At the Express & Star, deputy editor Derek Tucker studied the MoD press release and came across to my desk. "If there are press seats on that Hercules," he said, "we ought to be on it." In this case, as in so many conversations involving editors, "we" translates as "you."

I rang the MoD press desk where a plummy-voiced duty officer gave me what we call in journalese the thumbs-down, otherwise known as the red light.

"A press trip to Sarajevo?" he laughed gently. "I don't think so, old boy."

This old boy was mightily relieved. But in military PR nobody makes a decision without running it past his or her superior; it is called putting up your umbrella. By the time I got home that evening, the idea of putting some media types on the First Hercules into Sarajevo had reached ministerial level and been approved.

At 7pm my phone rang. It was the deputy features editor with a message from the MoD to be at RAF Lyneham the following morning with personal equipment for three days and a one-million dollar insurance waiver.

"What's that?" I asked.

"Haven't a clue," he said. "Good luck."

Twelve hours passed. At RAF Lyneham a group of about eight journalists gathered. My co siege-breakers included Barry Batchelor, the PA photographer, ITN's Michael Nicholson, reporters from the Daily Mail and the Scotsman, a BBC representative and one or two others. The sergeant in charge asked if we all had our personal kit for three days. We all nodded. "And the insurance waivers?" asked the sergeant. Again we all nodded.

"What's this waiver thing?" someone asked me.

"Haven't a clue," I ventured. "Just smile."

We flew to Zagreb from where, the following day, we would make the 75-minute hop into Sarajevo. We were in high spirits until that evening when, after we'd been issued with flak jackets and gathered around a trestle table, a senior UN official Mik Magnusson gave us a briefing on the current situation regarding the Serbs. He began: "If they let this flight through without shooting at it, it means there is enough humanity around to send a message to the people who claim to lead these factions that there is another way out."

It was fine, stirring stuff but none of us hacks had got beyond the word "if." We had assumed everything had been agreed with the Serbs. Apparently not. There was some sort of informal local truce but no-one seemed to have much faith in it.

"Maybe it would be an idea," said one of our minders, pushing his flak jacket away across the table, "if one of us stayed behind here in Zagreb, a sort of rear party. I don't mind volunteering." He was sort of joking.

One of the reporters pushed the flak jacket firmly back across the table and into the minder's chest. He was sort of joking, too.

I had a restless night four floors up in a big hotel near the centre of Zagreb. I woke early, washed, shaved and packed. Reporters like travelling light but sometimes you can't. There was the laptop computer, the notebooks, reference books (all pre-Google), the camera and spare lenses (all pre-digital) and that damned flak jacket.

As I left my room and stepped on the landing, so did Barry the photographer whose load, including a packed camera bag as well as that damned flak jacket, was twice mine.

"I'm going to have to wear this thing," said Barry, settling his baggage around him and pulling on the flak jacket.

"Me, too," I said, climbing into mine. It was heavy, hard and bulky but easier to wear than to carry.

Barry and I entered the empty lift and pressed the button for reception. The lift descended but halted at the next floor. The doors opened. Michael Nicholson of ITN was waiting to get in. Cool, steel-grey and on his umpteenth war, Nicholson was unflustered and unfettered. God knows where his kit was. He looked us up and down, we pair of provincial hacks in our rambling boots, anoraks and flak jackets, both trying to look cool and professional in the presence of a TV legend. Nicholson nodded at our flak jackets.

"Expecting trouble in reception, are we?" he smiled.

We took off at about 5.30am. As the RAF Hercules approached Sarajevo, I looked around at the other hacks. In the booming, gloomy belly of the transport aircraft, hunched on folding seats next to huge parcels of food and medicine, all looked glum. Some miles back we had each made our silent decision either to a) wear your flak jacket to protect the heart and vital organs from bullets striking the plane at an angle or b) sit on your flak jacket, in the manner of GIs in Vietnam, to protect the genitals from ground-shots directly below. Now, the engines throttled back. Eyes widened. Mouths turned dry. No-one spoke. We all sat deathly-still, as though moving around might catch that bullet you would otherwise avoid. Still, all still.

All, that is, except for one reporter who bounced around energetically in his seat, pen in one hand, sheaf of receipts and bar-chits in the other, searching his pockets for more paperwork, trying to make two plus two equal at least seven. Unruffled by the increasingly steep descent, untroubled by thoughts of bullets or shrapnel, he was following the first guiding principle of the ancient craft of journalism, the golden rule that applies whether you're covering a cat show in Stafford or doing the war-reporter thing and dropping like a stone into the shattered, starving, besieged and exceedingly dangerous capital of Bosnia: alive or dead, get your expenses sorted.

The nose dropped. There was a Stuka moment. On the airstrip at Sarajevo, the watching crowd included Martin Bell, the BBC legend in his "lucky" white suit. Some years later we met and he recalled that Hercules dropping like a stone on to the runway. "A real Khe Sanh landing," Bell called it, referring to Hercs in Vietnam using this same technique to avoid enemy guns at the Khe Sanh base. It looked startling to observers; those of us inside the Herc felt our ears pop and innards wobble. An impact, a rumble and we were down. We never knew if anyone had fired at us but some weeks later an Italian relief Hercules was brought down by Serb gunfire and there were no survivors.

The terminal at Sarajevo was the saddest place I had ever seen. Windows were shattered by gunfire. The floor, crunching beneath our feet, was carpeted in shards of broken glass and thousands of Kalashnikov cartridge cases. The place had been shot up, wrecked with gunfire by people with too many bullets and not enough brains. Yet on the counters, still open, were the booking forms, ticket stubs and boarding cards of a saner age. Here, frozen in time, was the moment when normality was overwhelmed by madness and the airport workers, without even closing their books, fled before the gunman. A Mary Celeste of airports. After our flight, this is what I wrote:

Sarajevo, July 3, 1992
The first British mercy flight into the shattered and starving city of Sarajevo touched down dramatically at exactly 7am British time today. The pilot of the RAF Hercules, Squadron Leader Chris 'Stingray' Tingay made a steep approach through a bank of dense clouds only 250ft above the bomb marked runway. Although a local ceasefire has been agreed, the rattle of small arms fire and the heavy thudding of mortar rounds could be clearly heard as we landed.

'It's great to see you, good to have you here – well done, the Brits,' said Commandant Raymond Hauben of the Belgian army who is in charge of United Nations flight control at Sarajevo airport.

As he spoke 40,000lb of desperately needed food, baby food and medicines were speedily loaded onto white UN cargo trucks for the high-speed dash into Sarajevo. The RAF flight, codenamed Operation Cheshire, was originally planned for yesterday but was delayed until a 1,000-strong Canadian infantry battalion made their way overland to secure the airport. It was a tense seventy-five-minute flight from Zagreb. The Hercules is unarmed apart from devices to jam radar and heat seeking missiles. We sat nervously inside the Hercules, wearing flak jackets.

From the air, Sarajevo, a town of 400,000 people looked utterly deserted. No one moved through the streets. At the airport terminal, peppered with mortar holes and strewn with debris, the group of French marines peered nervously through gunslits at a wasteland of burned out cars and shattered buildings where snipers had been seen earlier. A bullet hole inches above their positions told of an earlier near miss.

The full horror of what is happening in the Bosnian capital of Sarajevo was brought home by an army doctor, thirty-one-year-old Major Vanessa Lloyd-Davies, in charge of the airport's military hospital and a regular visitor.

'We have a nursing sister from a nearby village where they are eating grass because there is no food left. They haven't seen milk or baby food for days.'

Army medic Sergeant Geoff Newitt, a veteran of several army tours into the 'bandit country' of South Armagh said: 'Compared to Northern Ireland this is much more dangerous.'

The RAF Hercules will make a second flight into Sarajevo later today. As the international aid mission gathers pace, cargo aircraft are also arriving from America, Canada, and Norway. Although today's delivery was relatively small – armed forces minister Archie Hamilton yesterday described it as 'an important drop in the ocean' – it had great symbolic significance.

Although today's mission was a success, few observers here held much long term optimism. Mik Magnusson said he was depressed by the mutual hatred of all sides. Atrocities committed in the Balkans, he said, were worse than anything seen in Africa.

'The more cynical of us feel that a lot more blood will have to flow and be seen to flow before the international community reacts. These are poor peasant people and the world does not seem to see them dying.'

The strange part is that although every journalist on that Hercules reported what happened on the way in, there was little mention of our less-than-glorious departure from Sarajevo Airport. After the cargo was unloaded amid much back-slapping and goodwill, the pilot pressed the start button. The Hercules wouldn't start. Like a clapped-out old car it coughed unwillingly a few times and went quiet. The sun was rising. The Serb gunners in the hills would be awake. A Herc in the sunshine is a big, tempting target.

From the front of the plane, a young RAF technician moved quickly rearward, reaching over our heads to pull the plastic covers off the wiring loom and inserting short lengths of cable tipped with crocodile clips.

"Er, what are you doing?" I asked nervously.

"Just by-passing some of the safety circuits to give us enough power to start the motor," he explained.

"Is this normal procedure?" (Trying to sound inquisitive, not terrified).

"Yeah, sort of. The American version of this aircraft has a full toolkit for this sort of thing."

"And why doesn't the RAF version?"

The technician's reply has stayed with me ever since and I have heard it, or versions of it, repeated many times by soldiers, sailors and airmen.

"Because the MoD are a penny-pinching bunch of bastards," said the RAF lad. His fix worked. One engine started, followed by the other. The Herc, built to carry 40,000lbs of kit and now empty apart from a posse of scared hacks, went up like a rocket into the deep blue sky. After a minute or so the pilot tipped the nose forward and the profile of the curve created a moment of belly-wobbling weightlessness. One of the crewman, showing off for his civvy guests, spread his arms and flew for a few seconds in the rear of the hold, wide-eyed and smiling, like an angel in combat kit.

Vietnam – into the tunnels

In 1993 I was dispatched twice to Hong Kong, first in the spring at the invitation of the HK Government to promote the "business as usual" message as the 1997 deadline for handover to China grew closer and some jitters started. This was at the time when, after the chaotic and tragic exodus of "the Boat People" from Vietnam, some experts were predicting that thousands of wealthy Hong Kongers – inevitably dubbed "the Yacht People" – might desert the territory. This apocalyptic event never happened. Between them, London and Beijing maintained calm. As a government minister told me on an earlier visit: "If two ancient diplomatic powers like Britain and China can't do this, there is no hope in the world."

The second HK trip came in November and was simply a tourism trip with a few nights in HK and then on to Vietnam. On my two previous trips I'd been the stranger abroad. It was wonderful this time to have a local guide and to be shown the places I'd entirely missed before. At a Taoist temple one of our party asked to have his fortune told by a lined old soothsayer who duly delivered half-a-dozen platitudes and then charged him 20 dollars.

"Bet you didn't see that coming," we chorused.

Vietnam divided our eight-strong press party into two distinct groups. Four were under 40 and for them Vietnam was just a charming, hot, exotic tourist destination. But for the rest of us, of a certain age, this was history brought to life. We had grown up with Vietnam on the television every night from the first landings by US Marines to that final, panic-stricken flight in helicopters off the US Embassy roof. And here we were, among it all. Here, the old embassy, there the presidential palace where the North Vietnamese Army's tanks crushed the iron gates, bringing the war to an end. Inside the palace, tourists could have their photo taken in the presidential chair. Chris Buckland, the Fleet Street reporter who had won a certain fame with a snappy line from another conflict, settled into the giant leather seat and I took the photo.

Saigon, now renamed Ho Chi Minh City, was busy, friendly and cheap. We stayed in the Floating Hotel moored on the Mekong River, the only hotel I've ever stayed in where the wardrobes contained life jackets. Tourism was in its infancy and if the Saigon folk had seen quite enough Western men, they were fascinated by the women reporters in our group. In the Chinese quarter a group of women pointed and giggled and one of them approached our female guide and whispered to her. The guide looked mortified and blushed deeply.

"What is it?" we asked.

"These women," she explained haltingly. "Well, the thing is, they want to know, would it be permissible for them to touch the ladies' noses?"

To their credit, the women in our party stepped forwards, hooters presented for inspection, and the Chinese ladies, by now shaking with laughter and wonder, touched these amazing Western noses. A little blow for Anglo-Vietnam relations.

The highlight of our trip was the Tunnels of Cu Chi which I knew something about, having interviewed Tom Mangold in 1985 when he published his excellent book on the tunnels. Part of me wanted to see them but the other part dreaded the claustrophobia. Here we go…

November 1993

The tunnels of Cu Chi extend for about 200 miles. After ten yards I'd had enough. Ten feet underground the tunnel is so narrow it brushes your sides, so low you are bent double. The way both forward and back is blocked by other people. The tunnel widens into an old Vietcong conference room. It steadily fills with trippers until we are standing, sweating, shoulder to shoulder. The only way out is another panicky, heart-thumping crawl into the rat-run of tunnels. A bat suddenly flickers through the gloom. You duck. A woman gasps in alarm. Your chest tightens from belly to throat. Know the enemy. And if your darkest enemy is claustrophobia, then give the tunnels of Cu Chi a miss.

Yet even in the narrowest, lowest part of this section, you are not experiencing a fraction of the horrors of this place. Throw in the type of warfare that went on down here, the shooting, spearing, knife-fighting and booby traps, all in the pitch black, and you are into the stuff of nightmares. The tunnels on show today have been specially enlarged for the tourists. Originally they were scooped out, with trowel and wicker basket, no more than a couple of feet high. The slender jungle fighters of the Vietcong (VC) could slip through with ease; the big-boned Yanks stuck fast. At least that was the theory as the VC dug ever deeper and further. Eventually, the tunnels extended from the Cu Chi district, thirty miles north of Saigon, to the very gates of the city.

They are on three levels, the deepest more than thirty feet below ground. Armouries and operating theatres were constructed. Kitchens worked around the clock, the tell-tale smoke dispersed through a cunning colander of vents. See it here? Look again, smiles our Vietnam Army guide. Beneath a pile of leaves in the dappled jungle, a chimney barely as wide as a finger produces a thin trail of acrid blue smoke from the charcoal cooker below. Entrances were hidden beneath camouflaged steel trap doors or dug into river banks below river level. By day the Vietcong rested or sneaked out to work their paddy fields. By night, they emerged from their secret tunnels and gave the Yankees hell.

From the mid 1960s the US Army knew there were tunnels. But even the most intensive searches failed to find more than a few trapdoors, baited with landmines to kill the intruder. When the Yanks sent down sniffer dogs, the VC began using stolen US soap and combat jackets to hide their alien scent. The unfortunate US 25th Division unwittingly built its headquarters on top of the tunnels and suffered dreadful losses as the Vietcong emerged, machine-gunned the Americans' tents and blew up their helicopters.

The communists foraged for US weapons. After every air strike or artillery bombardment they would seek out unexploded shells and bombs, sawing them open, often with fatal consequences, to use the precious explosives in home-made grenades and rockets. They even perfected a mine, triggered by the swaying palm branches, to destroy helicopter gunships. So secure felt the VC that ceremonies were held underground to present medals to those who killed Americans and destroyed tanks. There were cultural events with dancers and singers smuggled down from North Vietnam to entertain the troops.

The US response was to form the Tunnel Rats, a volunteer unit of small, dedicated soldiers who braved the furthest recesses of this awful place to play 'Charlie' at his own game. See here, says the guide. In the corner of the underground command cell is a ten-foot pit, razor-sharp bamboo stakes in the bottom.

'When the American found a room, he always went into the corner. It was the best place to fight from. So we dug these,' the soldier smiles.

The Americans always tried to recover their dead or wounded Tunnel Rats, tugging them out with a rope around the feet. The Vietcong responded by lying in wait where the tunnels widened into rooms. As the Tunnel Rat stuck his head in, the waiting VC would skewer him through the neck with a bamboo spear, trapping the body forever. Other traps included grenades on trip wires and hollow tubes containing spiders, scorpions, poisonous snakes – and worse. There were many awful ways to die in 'Nam but could anything rival the agony and wretchedness of one Tunnel Rat, choked to death by a boa constrictor in a VC trap?

From the tunnels of Cu Chi, the Vietcong planned, equipped and launched their 1968 Tet offensive on Saigon and other major cities. Suddenly, the black-pyjama guerillas were everywhere. American television audiences awoke to see their own embassy in Saigon overrun by Vietcong.

At this stage fiction takes over from fact in the all-pervading propaganda dished out to today's thin but growing trickle of tourists. If you believe everything they tell you at Cu Chi, the Americans were defeated by a popular uprising among the people. It wasn't quite like that. The VC guerillas who streamed out of Cu Chi expected the city folk of Saigon to rally to their support. It didn't happen. Tet was a military disaster for the communists. The US Embassy takeover, described by one American officer as 'a piddling platoon action,' was repulsed in a matter of hours. The VC lost 40,000 dead in Tet and was so badly mauled that it never again fought a pitched battle.

Worse was to follow. Cu Chi was razed by huge US bulldozers, its trees stripped bare with defoliant chemicals. The US dropped tons of 'American grass' seed, producing a tinder-dry crop which was then ignited from the air. Cu Chi was declared a free-fire zone. Anything that moved was attacked.

Warplanes returning with unused bombs were told to drop them on Cu Chi. Finally, when the mighty B-52 bombers were no longer being used against the North, they set about carpet-bombing Cu Chi. Where the Tunnel Rats had failed, 1,000lb, delayed-action bombs succeeded. Vast sections of the maze were destroyed.

Of the sixteen thousand guerillas who fought from Cu Chi, ten thousand were killed. But that was not the point. The men and women who lived and died in these tunnels may have been beaten in military terms but they won an overwhelming victory for hearts and minds. For after Tet, the American public gave up all hope of winning the war. In the very week of the offensive, the tally of American dead in Vietnam passed that of the Korean War, traumatising the nation. In all, 50,000 Americans were to die here. The anti-war movement grew. Richard Nixon was elected on the pledge of bringing the boys home. Later the North Vietnamese Army, assisted by the remnants of the Vietcong, invaded the South and took over.

Today, the tunnels of Cu Chi are tranquil, surrounded by an eerie forest of saplings and American grass. The enemy's old bombs and shells are museum pieces. Bomb-craters are signposted and displayed with pride, like war wounds. And here and there, from vents deep-hidden in the leaf mould, come the gasps of tourists deep below. Amazement, admiration, panic.

Chris Buckland's memorable war quip? During the first Gulf War, billeted in a grand hotel, he rewrote the old adage about truth being the first casualty of war. His intro was: "The first casualty of war is not truth. It is room service."

To the North Pole (almost)

In the middle of May 1998 the phone rang at my desk in Wolverhampton. It was a local councillor, Phil Bateman.

"Hi, Pete," he announced. "Fancy going to the North Pole?"

"But of course. When?"

"Day after tomorrow?"

We met the next day outside the skiing-kit shop in Wolverhampton. It was closed. So we rustled together all the cold-weather kit we could cadge from friends and neighbours and, the very next day, flew out of Birmingham to Edmonton via New York and Toronto. It was all rather 19th century when an Englishman in a stout tweed jacket with a good pair of boots was a match for anything Mother Nature could chuck at him. Many sorrowful little cairns around the world tell another story.

The background to this trip was that a young explorer, Pen Hadow, was making his way from Resolute Bay in northern Canada to the North Pole. If he succeeded, it would be the first one-man expedition to the pole with no outside support. But things were going wrong. Hadow was marching 20 miles a day northwards across the frozen seas. But each night as he camped, the ice floes drifted southwards. It was like taking two steps up a staircase and one step down. Hadow was running low on supplies and, although the explorer didn't know it, Phil Bateman's job was to bring him home.

Hadow's epic trek was sponsored by the bus company National Express and Bateman, press officer for National

Express, was tasked with getting maximum publicity. I was not his first choice.

Ideally, Bateman would have been accompanied to the roof of the world by either ITV or BBC or one of the national newspapers. The snag was that while flights into Resolute Bay were fairly reliable, getting out again could be a problem if blizzards struck. It was not unusual for visitors to be stranded in the bleak little Inuit village for days on end. The prospect of having one precious film crew snowed in 5,000 miles away made television editors in London very jumpy. Then there was the risk factor.

"Bloody BBC said it would take two weeks for them to do a risk-assessment," Bateman told me later.

Fleet Street, as we still call it, was equally wary of dispatching their finest to the frozen north. And so, working down his wish-list, Bateman's finger landed on my name. I was not Kate Adie or John Simpson but as the chief feature writer on Britain's biggest-selling regional newspaper, also supplying copy and photos through a syndication agreement to the Press Association, I was the best he could find. And nobody in the E&S management seemed unduly worried about me being away for as long as it took.

From Edmonton we took a Boeing 737 via Yellowknife and Cambridge Bay into Resolute. The sun shone brightly through the next few days and nights. Time became meaningless. Your watch said 3.20 but which 3.20? The village was a collection of pastel-coloured pre-fab homes, hotel, school and a store which was resupplied twice a year when the sea thawed.

Resolute is about 74 degrees north on the globe. Pen Hadow was hundreds of miles away from us, trudging his lonely furrow towards the pole and now approaching 86 degrees north. We booked into the hotel where the locals chuckled at our ski suits and anoraks and led us off to a proper Arctic-equipment store. It looked like row after row of dead seals hanging on hooks. These were the sealskin Inuit trousers, jackets and boots, specifically designed to spare your friends the task of building a sorrowful little cairn in your memory.

The next day Phil and I plus a pilot and co-pilot, boarded a Twin Otter on ice skis and set off on the rescue mission. We covered 1,000 miles and were airborne for 14 hours, landing twice on the frozen sea to refuel from bright orange barrels of fuel, dumped strategically across the territory. I am not a happy flyer and this one seemed never-ending. At one stage somebody thought they had spotted a mighty musk ox. We swooped down to have a look. As we approached the black dot, we agreed it was not one musk ox but two. And they appeared to be mating. As the Twin Otter swept over we could positively identify this great creature. It was a rock.

We would never have found Pen Hadow by eyesight. The GPS tracker picked up his signal and the pilot began a long, slow descent, looking for a suitably flat patch of ice free of ravines and inlets. By this time I was planning my intro, the first paragraph of my report. Any news reporter will tell you the first par is the critical one. But reporters deal in short 200 or 250-word stories. A feature writer, to be successful, has to engage his reader and lead him through 1,000 words or more. So that first par becomes even more important. I had been toying with an historic line from another occasion when a journalist set out to find an explorer. When Stanley met Doctor Livingstone deep in the African bush he famously declared: "Dr Livingstone, I presume?" That would be my intro. I would reach out and deliver a firm handshake with the words: "Mr Hadow, I presume?"

But as the Twin Otter bumped through the clouds towards Hadow, an egg intervened.

"Anybody fancy an egg sandwich?" asked the co-pilot. I reached out. I was starving and an egg sarnie sounded grand. But it wasn't. It was soft boiled and wobbly and neither hot nor cold but somewhere in between, at about blood temperature. I chewed and, against my better judgment, swallowed it down. To my credit, I hung on to that egg sandwich for fully 10 minutes. We landed. Pen Hadow came bouncing over the ice like an enthusiastic labrador puppy. I extended my hand to the great man and announced: "Mr Heeuurrgh," and threw up. I swear that egg sandwich was frozen solid before it hit the ice. Bang goes the Dr Livingstone intro.

We were at 86 degrees North, a couple of hundred miles short of the pole. It was fiercely sunny and the ice, even shielded by a pair of sunglasses topped with a US Army anti-glare visor, was painfully bright. The temperature was minus 20C but the air was dry and it felt no colder than a good English snow scene. Hadow was in great spirits although he admitted that might have been related to the painkillers he had been chewing since twisting an ankle a few days before. It was some minutes before he realised what Phil Bateman was saying, namely that he'd put up a good show and they were all proud of him but it was time to come home.

Pen Hadow was not prepared to give up. He refused to be rescued.

"Game on," he insisted brightly. All we could do was leave him with extra food and a tiny folding boat to cope with the stretches of black, deadly-cold water gradually intruding into the ice floes. We flew back to Resolute Bay. Pen Hadow trudged on for a few more days and was eventually rescued by the Canadian Navy.

Phil Bateman and I, with a day to spare before the plane to Edmonton was due, accepted an invitation from the Mayor of Resolute, the late Gary Guy, to join him on a seal hunt out on the frozen sea. Bateman, ever the politician, made it clear that he would not even touch the rifle, let alone kill anything. I took the view that the village dogs were hungry, the community needed seal meat and, as a good shot in the TA, I could do the job. The hunt began, the three of us on snowmobiles, Guy towing a timber sled for the piles of seal we were about to slay and me carrying the bolt-action hunting rifle. After a few miles we halted. The glare off the ice was almost unbearable.

"Remember," said the Mayor, "if you see anything black, it's a seal."

I scoured the horizon. There was no shortage of black things but they were all floaters in my own eyes, magnified by the ice glare and moving around in lazy circles behind the lens. I was looking for something black, solid and stationary. And there it was. It was big. It was black. It was an easy shot, no more than a couple of hundred yards away. There was no telescopic sight on the rifle but the precision fixed sights were fine. I began to draw a bead on Blackie, the soon-to-be-late seal. Suddenly there was a hand on my shoulder.

"Do not shoot that," said Gary Guy.

"Why not? It's black. It's a seal."

"No, it isn't. It's my boat. It's a converted landing craft and it's at least five miles away."

Welcome to the distorting factor of gin-clear Arctic skies that make judging distance almost impossible. From time to time, Guy told us later, trippers would set off from Resolute Bay to walk a couple of miles to an island in the frozen bay. The island was actually 53 miles away.

No seals perished in the making of this story. We didn't see a single one, black or otherwise, but we did find a hole in the ice where a family of seals had gathered before hearing the distant hum of the snowmobiles and slipping into the sea. Little frozen stains of yellow urine marked where they had rested. So like us.

On the way back to Resolute we skirted a ravine and my snowmobile began yawing left and right as I oversteered. Eventually I hit the edge of the gulley and, as the snowmobile went one way, I went another, describing an elegant parabola before coming to earth. In the split second before landing I saw a snowdrift and thought, in my English suburban way: "Well, that'll be a nice, soft landing." As a rule a snowdrift is soft. But not when it's been there for 10,000 years. It was like iron and I flew home to Britain a couple of days later with a leg swollen like a marrow.

Years later, in 2017, Pen Hadow set off on yet another polar mission. I wrote this:

"In May 1998, for reasons I won't tire you with, I was standing on an ice floe 200 miles from the North Pole at 20 degrees below zero, watching a councillor from Wolverhampton trying to persuade an Arctic explorer to pack it in and come home (like I say, it's complicated). The explorer, Pen Hadow, was making absolutely no progress on his way to the pole. But, despite the pain, cold and polar bears, he refused to be rescued. All we could do, after a perilous 14-hour flight to find him, was give him extra food and a small boat and wish him well. Now, at 55, he's off again, leading a party trying to sail two yachts to the pole to demonstrate climate change. Back in '98 he struck me as slightly bonkers and a tad selfish. But above all, a tiny dot at the top of the world, limping on with an injured knee, he looked incredibly vulnerable. I would not have put money on him being alive, let alone still exploring, nearly 20 years later. Bon voyage, you clot."

A feline footnote

Back in Resolute Bay, Gary and his wife had a pair of Maine Coone cats, the biggest domestic cats in the world. They were supposed to join us on the last night of our adventure for roast-chicken supper but one (let us call him Bad Cat) was in disgrace, having killed and eaten a snow bunting. The poor bunting, killed and dismembered on the veranda, probably had no idea what a cat was. The Guys found Bad Cat surrounded with blooded feathers and locked him in the porch for the duration while his brother (let us call him Good Cat) settled, like a big, furry Buddha into the armchair at the head of the table with the humans. He was thoroughly spoiled. We stroked him, tickled his ears and fed him little pieces of chicken throughout the meal. And when the meal was ended, Mrs Guy put down a saucer of gravy which Good Cat lapped enthusiastically. We drank and chatted and reflected on an extraordinary few days. We raised a toast to the distant Pen Hadow, still slogging through eternal sunshine on his doomed trek northwards. And then there was a sort of gurgling, retching noise in the corner of the room as Good Cat was spectacularly sick. Out came the gravy, then the pieces of chicken. And then the snow bunting. We were shocked. Bad Cat was not so bad after all. It was Good Cat who had not only killed the snow bunting and eaten it but framed his own brother for buntingcide. Never put your faith in cats. They will always let you down.

A night to remember

A great strength of the Express & Star was its team of feature writers, given a wide brief to produce in-depth features and opinion pieces on the events of the day. The briefing would usually be on the lines of: "Don't cover the big event, there's a reporter already there. Give us the background, the colour, the off-guard comments and asides." Here's an example from that memorable General Election night in 1997 when Blairism swept the board with a Labour landslide. Nowhere was safe for the Tories, not even Enoch Powell's old seat, Wolverhampton South-West, where the long-serving Tory MP, Nick Budgen was ousted by Labour's Jenny Jones. It was a night of history and a reminder of how brutal a game is politics. The year after this trauma Nick Budgen died of cancer. Jenny Jones, who had never expected to win the seat, hated Westminster and resigned in 2001 after one term. No-one in the Civic Hall that night will forget it.

AN HOUR before it was officially declared, you could see the result in the body-language. The terrible stillness of Nicholas Budgen and his Tory supporters was an abiding image of Wipeout '97.

In contrast, Jenny Jones, Labour's woman in Wolverhampton South-West, and her fans were excited, animated. They touched and chattered. Budgen and Co sat, slumped, arms folded defensively.

As they climbed the steps to the Civic Hall stage, Jones held her hands low in front of her, like a rather excited head teacher about to announce a Very Special Occasion. Budgen stood ashen faced, hand behind his back, like a man awaiting the firing squad, framed between potted begonias and miniature palms.

No-one in the hall heard the full result. Nicholas Budgen got 19,539 votes. Jenny Jones got 24,000 and something but the roar of the crowd drowned out the hundreds, tens and units of victory.

Her speech was a headmistress sort of speech. She stood, and sounded, like Joyce Grenfell: 'I want to thank all the staff who have had a very long day.'

Nicholas Budgen was barracked by Labour's yobbish tendency but pressed on. It was the right stuff for such occasions. Splendid battle, friendship, vigour, the ups and downs of politics, our time will come, etc etc. (Later, he was overheard asking an aide: 'Was the bullshit all right?')

In truth, the end of his time had come, and come like a thunderbolt. Nicholas Budgen is a cold fish, quite unsuited to, and unhappy with, the flesh-pressing, baby-kissing demands of modern campaigning.

While other wannabee MPs grinned and gawped for the cameras, Nick Budgen slunk into the background like a vampire at a garlic festival.

When his aides insisted he be seen at a Wolves match, he gritted his teeth and went. Duty before pleasure. During the match (it is alleged) a mighty roar went up from Molineux. 'Either Wolves have scored,' quipped a Tory aide, 'or they've lynched him.'

In a campaign dictated by Tony Blair and fought on touchy-feely niceness rather than policies, Budgen had the bad luck to come up against Jenny Jones.

A plump, huggable wife and mum, steeped in local politics, a school governor and health council member, she works as a small-business adviser and has the disarming ability to baby-talk with toddlers one minute and debate the intricacies of Keynesian economics the next.

Budgen responded by playing the race card and invoking the spirit of his illustrious predecessor, Enoch 'Rivers of Blood' Powell.

It was a high-risk strategy. Powell got it wrong. Powell got the sack. Budgen got it wrong. Budgen got the sack, too. As the feely-huggy brigade cheered Jenny Jones, a great roar went up, like a pack baying at the kill.

And they reflected on how easily they had flushed out, and culled, the fox-hunting barrister in Wolverhampton South West. Tallyho.

Hedgehogs and narrowboats

In March 2003, the strangest assignment came my way. Five hundred and fifty miles north of Wolverhampton, the Hebridean island of Benbecula was the setting for man's inhumanity to hedgehogs. The wee beasties, through no fault of their own, had been introduced in the 1970s to keep down the local slugs and thus protect the islanders' precious vegetable crops. But the hedgehogs quickly discovered another source of protein, courtesy of the local gulls and other seabirds which nested and laid their eggs on the tussocky ground between meadows and shoreline. The hogs grew fat, and also developed a fetching shade of blonde, on a diet of eggs. With the bird population at threat, the authorities ordered a cull of the hedgehogs. But a period of grace was announced before the hunters arrived with their shotguns and lethal injections.

A frantic race began to trap, save and export the hogs to the mainland. By now, all newspapers were facing tight budgets and there was little direct Black Country interest in the Hebrides cull. But the new editor, Adrian Faber, recognised a heart-warming tale, even if it would cost us a few hundred pounds, and dispatched me and a photographer, Gavin Dickson, to Benbecula, via Skye where we broke the journey with a fish and chip lunch by the harbour at the island's pastel-painted capital, Portree. In my life I have had three memorable portions of fish and chips, the first sitting on the sea wall at Whitby, the second sitting on the sea wall at Portree and the third sitting on the sea wall at Lyme Regis. It makes me think there is more to great fish and chips than merely chips and fish. The sea wall is as essential to perfect fish and chips as vinegar or a mug of tea.

A bonnie boat, in the shape of the island ferry, took us across to Benbecula with its white-sand beaches and emerald shores. These are some of the most beautiful beaches in the United Kingdom and yet they are usually deserted, probably because there are so few hotels or guest houses. Gavin and I had a couple of rooms in a little B&B and went out on two nights to hunt the hogs with the rescuers. With torches and cotton bags, they were doing a fine job and had gathered dozens of the creatures into a portable clinic where they were weighed, measured and, if damaged, patched up. They were fed on what looked like cat food and the clinic, stuffed with volunteers, hogs, old blankets and meat, smelt exactly as you'd expect.

I sometimes wonder how many of those hedgehogs survived the transition to the mainland where, over the next 20 years, hedgehog numbers would plummet. With hindsight, did the welfare of Hebridean sea birds really matter more than a thriving colony of endearing little mammals? The only justification I ever heard was that the seabirds were native species while the hedgehogs were alien. It is strange how we enforce immigration rules against animals that no decent person would dream of imposing on humans.

Back home, a few weeks later, I was sent on a job that looked suspiciously like a jolly. Adrian Faber was fascinated by the industrial heritage of the Black Country. Like any true Brummie, Faber was aware that Birmingham had more miles of canals than Venice. So for that matter was the entertainer Clive Anderson who, in an after-lunch speech in the city, made the point that the difference is that while Venice's canals are full of gondolas, Birmingham's canals are full of shopping trolleys.

I was sent "up the cut" for a week in a 70ft narrow boat (never call them barges), filing daily dispatches as I went. My crew was provided by a succession of my neighbours, and photographers came out to join us every day. "A Black Country Voyage," as the series of features and the later book were called, was one of the most enjoyable assignments and the readers loved it, watching out for us and waving as our narrowboat Rosie pop-popped past. It was an opportunity to write from the heart and chuck in a little lyricism as we progressed from Penkridge to Wolverhampton, to Walsall and down to Kinver: *"The secret world of inland waterways opened unto us, narrowboats gliding by and the air reeking of warm grease and sulphurous coal."*

Jerome K Jerome, author of Three Men in a Boat, was born in Walsall and my watery epic was a little tribute to him. It was a blissful few days.

A couple of weeks later (as my brother put it when he had the same experience), my bloody eye fell out. It was a detached retina. My mother and two of my five brothers had the same problem so it's probably in the genes. But while they described a black curtain descending, mine was no more than a watery wobble, low in the vision of my right eye. Thankfully, it was caught early. The first operation seemed successful but, after a few weeks back in the office, it went wrong. The procedure eventually worked but only after a string of five more operations. Half-blind, I was off work for six months, writing and filing my daily E&S column, hiking the text size on the computer screen from 12 point to a whopping 72 point.

For a Shilling a Day

I returned to work just before Christmas 2003 and worked in Wolverhampton for the next nine years. But things were changing. There were some good assignments including a fishing weekend in Scotland and a memorable cruise down the Baltic from Estonia to Denmark. But most of my old colleagues had left, through retirement or voluntary redundancy and, as the internet advanced, our circulation was falling and editions were reduced.

But there was one project I was determined to finish. In 1998 I had published a slim volume of memories of warfare, interviews with old soldiers I'd carried out over the past 20 years. It was entitled *For a Shilling a Day: Black Country Memories of Warfare* and was well received. But as the years passed and I spoke to more veterans of the two world wars and other conflicts, including dozens from the 1982 Falklands War, it occurred to me that this compilation had more than local interest. In 2010 I published a second edition entitled simply: *For a Shilling a Day.* After generous reviews in the Daily Mail and British Journalism Review ("You can almost smell the cordite – and the blood") it sold well, rising in the Amazon charts to become the 42nd best-selling book, briefly displacing Barack Obama's autobiography.

But it wasn't about big sales. It was about getting these memories down before it was too late. The First World War generation had fallen off their perches, many taking their memories to the grave. One year there were plenty of WW1 survivors, the next a handful, and then they were gone.

Compiling war stories gave me an opportunity to research the death of my grandfather's brother Private Alvin Smith who died on the Somme in 1916. It was a poignant tale of a brave young man winning his sweetheart's respect. I had always assumed Alvin was killed by enemy guns.

Between the first and second editions of the book I uncovered a darker truth. He was, in all probability, killed by British mortars. At first I relied for my research into Alvin's death on *The West Riding Territorials in the Great War*, the authorised and approved version published in the 1920s. It carried an account of "this little action," the attack by the 1/7th Battalion Duke of Wellington's Regiment (West Riding) on trenches to the south of Thiepval on Sunday, September 17, 1916. But it was obvious that the writers, while dwelling in great detail on the packs and equipment carried by every man, were not telling the whole truth.

From family and other sources I knew that Alvin had been blown to bits and that his remains and those of his pals were found by a comrade who had gone back to replenish their water bottles. This was puzzling because, as a TA soldier, I knew that replenishing water and ammunition is a drill carried out before the battle, not after it had started. I knew, too, that a Military Cross had been awarded to Captain Basil Lupton for his heroism in standing on the trench parapet and rallying his men. Inexplicably, Lupton is not even mentioned in the official history. Strangest of all was the recollection, by an old uncle of mine, that the battalion, having fought like lions and won a remarkable victory in this, their first attack, refused to go on parade the following morning and threw their rifles to the ground. It was not a serious mutiny. Order was restored in a few minutes. Even so, it was hardly the behaviour you would expect from a battalion whose fine performance was to be marked by a visit from General Gough, the army commander himself. It did not make sense, until I went to the regimental museum at Halifax and ploughed through the battalion diaries, written in the field by a young officer shortly after the attack. The dark secret, pointedly ignored by the official history, was that in the minutes before the West Riding lads put in their attack, mortar bombs from their own trench-mortar battery fell at two places on the trench map, points 45 and 68, causing "a number of casualties." At point 45 it must have been hell on earth for, by a million-to-one chance, the shells detonated the battalion's supply of hand grenades. The effects of that sudden cataclysm of multiple explosions among men massed in trenches for an attack do not bear thinking about. The attack was a great success and the Dukes advanced 130 yards further than they had been ordered. But they lost 222 men killed or injured – about one-third of the total. Gradually the 80-year fog of deception cleared.

The final part of the jigsaw was, where was Alvin Smith during this affair? In 2010 the website *Craven's Part in the Great War* reproduced a letter from one of Alvin's comrades, referring to his chums from the Yorkshire village of

Lothersdale in C Company. From the battalion diary we knew that C Company was deployed at and around point 68, where the mortar bombs came whistling down. It seems likely that Alvin was killed by British mortars before the attack began.

The battalion succeeded but at a terrible cost, largely inflicted by their own side. Suddenly, you begin to understand why those bitter, terribly depleted ranks were in no mood for a parade, why they threw their Lee-Enfields to the ground. This "blue-on-blue" tragedy may also account for the fact that Alvin's family rarely spoke about his death.

Poor Captain Lupton didn't even get a mention in the approved history. But then how could the writers mention Lupton rallying the men under fire without mentioning that the fire was British? I was delighted, in later correspondence to learn that Basil Lupton, the heroic young officer who rallied his men after the mortar blasts by leaping on to the parapet, went on to be awarded the Military Cross for his bravery at Thiepval. With great irony, the citation refers to "very heavy fire," without explaining that it was British mortar fire. In another attack in 1918, Lupton earned a bar to his MC, in effect a second MC. I assumed someone so brave would never have seen the end of hostilities. So in 2011 I was pleased to learn that he survived the war and in the 1920s was living comfortably in a large house in Ilkley. Here is Alvin's story:

Lothersdale, North Yorkshire, Friday

THIS is where it began, in a Yorkshire village where the Smiths had farmed for generations. At Christmas 1915, Alvin Smith, the nineteen-year-old son of farmer Edmund and Sarah Jane Smith was walking with his girlfriend, Amy. The First World War had been raging for more than a year. Alvin's brother, John, (my grandfather) had joined up at the start. But Alvin had been needed to help run Burlington Farm. His dad insisted. It was an embarrassing position. All the best chaps seemed to be in khaki. It would not take much to make Alvin defy his parents. At Christmas it came.

'Would you love me if I was a soldier?' Alvin joked as he walked with Amy.

'Well,' teased the pretty eighteen-year-old, in a reply which was to haunt her for the next 80 years, 'I might respect you a bit more.'

Respect. That did it. Over Christmas dinner with friends and family, Alvin turned to his best pal, Willie Smith, and said: 'We'd better enjoy this Christmas, Willie, because we probably won't see the next one.'

'There was nothing dramatic about the way he said it,' Amy told me many years later. 'It was just a statement of fact.'

Alvin and Willie enlisted together on January 29, 1916, as privates in the Duke of Wellington's Regiment (West Riding). They were innocents in arms, rushed over to France after a frantic few weeks of training to take part in the long awaited British offensive which was already being called The Big Push. Soon, it would be known by a name which would become a byword for slaughter. The Somme.

Thiepval, The Somme, Sunday

THIS is where it ended, a placid corner of northern France where the autumn sun blazes down on dry, new-ploughed fields and the potato harvest is piled in tons beside the farm tracks. The scars of the 1916 trenches can still be seen and every year's ploughing uncovers the 'iron harvest' of unexploded shells. A few years ago, walking the route that Private Alvin Smith and his pals followed, I found something white sticking out of the earth bank of a sunken track. As I pulled it, eighteen inches of human thigh bone emerged, a reminder of the carnage on these gentle chalk slopes. In 1916 the Germans held the high ground here, commanding every hill-top and valley slope. The village of Thiepval and the 1,000-yard-long Thiepval Spur which stuck like a giant finger into the British lines were bristling with concrete gun emplacements, trenches and deep dugouts, all screened behind vast hedges of barbed wire. Alvin's battalion, the 1st/7th, was in reserve on the terrible First Day of the Somme on July 1, 1916, and was spared the horror which left 20,000 young Britons dead and 40,000 wounded. Alvin's friend, Willie Smith, was reported killed on July 7.

The Division got its first blooding in an attack on September 3. It failed wretchedly. The British commander-in-chief, General Sir Douglas Haig, was furious. He wrote scathingly in his diary: 'The total losses of this division are less than 1,000!' In the grim arithmetic of the Somme, where every yard was measured in deaths, the West Riding lads were not dying quickly enough. To infuriate the top brass further, some of the division's troops had failed to salute a visiting general, which probably explains the terse entry in the 1st/7th Battalion's diary for September 8: 'Games before breakfast followed by saluting drill.'

On September 15 another Yorkshire battalion seized German trenches south of Thiepval. Three companies of Alvin's battalion, about 600 men, moved forward that night to take over the trenches and prepare for another attack. It began, disastrously, at 6pm on Sunday, September 17, with a terrible misjudgment. The battalion's mortars got the range wrong and hit their own trenches, exploding a store of hand grenades. Amid the dead and wounded and the confusion of this 'friendly fire' incident, a Captain Lupton calmly climbed on to the trench parapet and heroically rallied the men. The attack was all over in an hour. It was such a success that General Gough visited the battalion two days later to offer his congratulations. The West Riding lads had advanced 350 yards beyond their objective. In doing so they lost 220 men. The arithmetic of the Somme was working. They never found Alvin's body. One of his mates went back for water and when he returned, the trench and its occupants had been blown to shreds. For years I assumed he had been killed by German guns but the more I researched, the more it became clear that Alvin Smith and his mates were probably killed before the attack even began, by their own side in the 'friendly fire' incident as the Stokes mortars fell short. Alvin was in C Company which was deployed around point 68 on the map, one of the places where, according to the battalion diary, the mortars fell. We will probably never know for sure.

The name of Private Alvin Smith is recorded on the Thiepval memorial to those who died on the Somme and who have no known grave. There are 73,000 names. A few days after his death, the local newspaper in Yorkshire recorded: 'He was well known in the village and district and was highly esteemed by all who knew him. He was a well-built youth, of a pleasant and cheerful disposition.'

Of all the many war stories I have collected, two from the First World War stick in my mind because they illustrate a simple truth of warfare, that there is no consensus, only a vast spread of human experiences and recollections.

The first was told to me by Fred Barnfield, a self-taught artist in the Black Country whose portraits in paint speckled on to canvas earned him the title "The Wednesbury Blobber." He joked that he was a drag artist – he had to drag people into his exhibitions. He had a passion for horse racing and in the 1960s would attend many meetings with an old friend called Dave, a Great War veteran whose fighting days had ended when his arm was sliced off by a shell splinter on the Western

Front. One summer evening, Fred and Dave were returning from Cheltenham Races and stopped for a drink on a hill overlooking a vast plain of chequered meadows. The sun was setting, the cornfields were gilded. They agreed it was a beautiful sight. And then Fred asked David: "What's the most beautiful thing you've ever seen?" Without a moment's hesitation the old soldier replied: "My arm, lying on the ground in France, because it meant I could go home." There are no words to describe the trauma and terror that make a young man positively welcome the loss of his arm. And if that was the only First World War story you ever heard, no-one could blame you for signing up to the Lions Led by Donkeys version.

The other story concerns Aubrey Moore whose fine memoir, *A Son of the Rectory,* was published in 1982. He was in his ninetieth year and his book was reckoned to be the last account of active service produced by a front-line officer of 1914-18.

Moore was tall, sparky and bright as a button, but also sensitive and thoughtful. As an officer in a tunnelling company, laying mines beneath the German trenches, he endured some terrible experiences and the loss of many good friends. Aubrey Moore ends his book with a description of an incident in a sap below enemy positions in 1915 which I defy anyone to read without shedding a tear. One Sunday evening the young officer went to the head of the sap and found Jabez Emerson, an NCO and an old school friend, on listening watch:

"We talked for a time and I saw he had a prayer book in his hand. He told me his people would about now be in chapel, so he was going through the evening service with them. We were eight or ten feet beneath a German trench full of soldiers and I could not help thinking about what their immediate thoughts were. How utterly incongruous the whole thing was."

Surely someone capable of such empathy would share the traditional view of the Great War as a wretched and terrible trauma? Not a bit of it. When he mentioned the Somme, he must have caught the flicker of sadness that crossed my face and was determined to stamp his beliefs on this interview.

"The war wasn't gloomy," he declared. "It makes me so wild to hear people talking or writing about the grumbling or the morale among troops. That is all rot. You can't really say there were blunders; you must remember that no-one had fought a war like that before. Mobilisation was a tremendous experience. We were all worried sick that the war would be over before we got into it! I'll say I enjoyed the war. It might have been just another blinking great cricket match. But of course, we were only children."

Celebrities – real-life and latex

With *For a Shilling a Day* published, I resumed the normal routine of writing leaders, my daily column (later reinvented as a blog) and general feature writing. By the nature of the job, this involves a lot of celebrities at varying levels of stardom or political fame. As a golden rule of such interviews, the best ones are the ones you expect to be a nightmare while the worst ones are those you thought would be a doddle.

If you are in journalism for 50 years, never being distracted into subbing or management (I always avoided any job with the word "editor" in the title), you can rack up an astonishing number of conversations. In my case, from 1969 to the present, it's about 12,000 interviews and eight million words. Some of those interviews were brief chats on the phone, others were much longer, like the three hours I spent facing the Sinn Fein leader Gerry Adams over a dining table in London at his first book launch as he crossed the divide from politics to celebrity. One question provoked a long, embarrassing silence. As I wrote:

When Gerry Adams suggests (over the cheese course), that Sinn Fein might settle, initially, for something less than the united Ireland dreamed of by every Republican since 1921, you begin to feel some pity for him. For when the legendary IRA leader Michael Collins signed the treaty with Britain and accepted a divided Ireland all those years ago, he also signed his own death warrant and was duly shot by his old IRA cronies. Does Adams worry about the assassin's bullet? For seven long seconds he says nothing. Then: 'I've already lived longer than Michael Collins.' As we pack up, Gerry Adams beams broadly. He thinks we have got on really well. 'You were combative,' he smiles, approvingly, signing the book. Despite myself, I shake his hand again and wish him well. Better the devil you know.

Other celebrities were encountered on the job. For a few months in the mid-1980s, a tousle-headed Oxford graduate joined the Express & Star in order to get a taste of the real England, beyond the M25. He stood out in his expensive pinstripe suits and seemed permanently puzzled, although agreeable enough. It was the young Boris Johnson.

Most interviews will be with people who could not be described as famous who are simply enjoying, or enduring, their 15 minutes of fame. But hundreds will have been touched by the strange thing we call celebrity, a breed apart from the rest of us. Some of them even refer to us ordinary folk as "civilians."

I sat down one afternoon in 2020 and, allowing myself 20 minutes, typed the names of the celebrities I'd interviewed who sprang to mind. I was booked at a public-speaking session and the idea was simply to read out the list and let the audience decide whom they wanted to know more about. And here's the roll-call. It is by no means a complete list, simply those I remembered first. This is pure name-dropping:

Val Doonican
Ozzy Osbourne
Michael Heseltine
Enoch Powell
Sally Burton
Pamela Stephenson
Wendy Craig
David Troughton
David Tennant
Patrick Stuart
William Shatner
Sir Ian McKellen
Gary Wilmot
Monica Lewinsky
Charlie Kray
John Major
Gordon Brown
Jack Straw
Tony Blair
Princess Anne
Jerry Marsden (of the Pacemakers)
Duke of Edinburgh
Henry Cooper
Frank Bruno
Brian Conley
Ulrika Johnsson
Britt Ekland

Linda Lusardi

Kenneth Williams

Anita Dobson

Frances de la Tour

Alan Bates

Adrian Edmondson

Phil Drabble

Ben Elton

Tony Benn

Bruce Kent

David Jenkins (Bishop of Durham)

Gennadi Gerasimov (Gorbachev's spokesman)

Jimmy Carter

Michaela Strachan

Matthew Kelly

Tom Wilkinson

Ted Allbeury

Chapman Pincher

Simon Callow

Cathy Tyson

Richard Dreyfuss

Hillary Mantel

Bob Newhart

John Humphrys

Bill Giles

Patrick Moore

Kenneth Branagh

Emma Thompson

Richard Briers

Barbara Dickson

Jo Brown and the Bruvvers

Gilbert O'Sullivan

Gary Glitter

Lord Carrington

Jon Snow

Martin Bell

Matt Lucas

David Walliams

Tom Mangold

Frank Skinner

Geoff Hamilton

Robin Cousins

Ruth Madoc

Peter Butterworth

Les Dawson

John Cleese

Denis Healey

John Smith

Gerry Adams

Billy Power & Hugh Callaghan (two of the Birmingham Six)

Lionel Jeffries

Bob Newhart

Nick Owen

Pen Hadow, explorer

Lenny Henry

Simon Weston

Andrew Davies

Val Singleton

Anne Diamond

Richard Attenborough

The Chuckle Brothers

Lionel Blair, plus his Dancers

And The entire cast of The Muppets

The hardest celebrity interview was one which, on paper, should have been dead easy. Sally Burton, widow of the great actor Richard Burton, was touring the country to promote Melvyn Bragg's biography of her late husband. As the standfirst, the brief par that introduces a feature, on my piece put it: *She claims it is the definitive biography. Others see it as yet another round in the battle between Sally Burton and Elizabeth Taylor. Peter Rhodes strayed into the crossfire.* Crossfire, indeed. My offence was to suggest that any biography of Richard Burton that did not include a single quote from Liz Taylor was, to put it mildly, odd. But worse than that in Sally's eyes, some weeks before I had interviewed Burton's younger brother, Graham Jenkins, who had published his memoirs of the superstar. Jenkins claimed that Burton did not want his diaries published until 20 years after his death. Sally Burton denounced the book as tacky. She accused Jenkins of a "get the widow'" vendetta and accused me of being "coloured" by meeting Jenkins. And then Sally Burton did something no other interviewee has done to me. She averted her eyes, stared at the wall and simply refused to say anything. I could do nothing but invite her to dictate exactly what she wanted to see in the paper. She said: "I would rather have married Richard Burton with all the excitement and the dangers than to have lived with someone bland. Any man who reads this book will wish Richard had been his friend and any woman who reads it will fall in love with him." Thank you, Mrs Burton, and good afternoon.

If Sally Burton was a difficult interview, Richard Attenborough, against the odds, was one of the best. He was coming to Birmingham in 1998 to lay the foundation stone of a new cinema and I was dispatched to interview him. I set off, glumly. Lord Attenborough was a giant of the arts, the luvvie's luvvie.

I told myself – and the features editor – that there wasn't a cat in hell's chance of getting anywhere near the great man, let alone asking a question. Sure enough, the place was rammed with bigwigs, hacks and adoring fans, all desperate to meet Dickie. I found myself next to him at the buffet, picking up chicken drumsticks.

"All well?" I asked.

"I feel old," said Attenborough, then 74. He explained that he'd recently been directing Pierce Brosnan in the movie Grey Owl, high up in the Canadian mountains. He felt young enough in spirit and his face looked young but his legs found all those snow drifts tiring.

"My father," I told him, "used to say that whenever he looked in a mirror, right into his sixties, he saw the face of a 17-year-old Bevin Boy looking back." The effect on Attenborough of this recollection, from a conscripted teenage coal miner of his own generation, was startling. It was as though someone had flicked a switch.

"That's exactly how it is!" he exclaimed. And for the next few minutes it was as though we were the only people in the room. He went on to say that the face looking back at him in the mirror each morning was that of the 17-year-old stoker from his first film in 1942, In Which We Serve. And he talked about his lifelong dream of making a film about Grey Owl, a native American who, in the 1930s, became a huge celebrity. In buckskins and full war bonnet, Grey Owl would thrill newspapers readers and theatre audiences with his warnings about the need to conserve species in northern Canada and to preserve their habitat. He was years ahead of his time. Attenborough told me how, as boys in 1936, he and his brother David queued for hours to see one of Grey Owl's lectures and the magical effect it had on them both.

This was turning into a rare insight into the influence that would later turn David Attenborough into the world's best known television naturalist and a global leader of the burgeoning movement to save the planet.

And the enormous irony, as Richard Attenborough recalled with a huge laugh, was that Grey Owl did not even exist. The "Red Indian" who captured so many imaginations was a fraud called Archie. Born in Hastings, Archibald Belaney had personal problems and alcohol issues and took himself off to the Canadian outback where he reinvented himself as Grey Owl, a member of the First Nation. It was a deception but a harmless one. He told lies but he also told a great truth and in 1997 the Mayor and Corporation of Hastings unveiled a blue plaque in his honour at the house where he was born.

Great interview. Wonderful story. And all that from an unpromising assignment about a new cinema in Brum.

There are dozens of actors in my list, partly because my brief included the Royal Shakespeare Company and its productions at Stratford. Most actors are down-to-earth types, only too happy to talk at whatever level they find themselves, whether it's a chat with a local newspaper or a four-page interview for Vogue. But from time to time you meet one so self-obsessed, so convinced the world revolves around them, that you can only keep on scribbling your notes and hope it will soon be over. In over 50 years as a hack one luvvie interview stands out from all the others. Firstly, this lady was not only unbearably pompous, but also a blatant and unashamed liar. Secondly, she was not flesh and blood. She was latex. She was Miss Piggy. She was terrific.

The Muppets came to town in 1992 to launch The Muppet Christmas Carol movie and I got to interview them in a suite at a hotel in Birmingham. It began with an informal chat with the performers, Brian Henson, Frank Oz, Steven Whitmire and Dave Goelz. Their puppets, lying on a sofa, were no more than colourful chunks of rubber and sticks. And then Oz picked up Miss Piggy and I asked her whether she was disappointed not to have more lines in the movie.

What happened next went beyond puppetry. It was like life itself. As I wrote at the time: *"The bald man with the deep voice suddenly speaks in a strident falsetto. Miss Piggy is made flesh."*

"As long as I'm with Kermit, it doesn't matter," the pig simpered. And off we went on our very own private Muppet Show, a spontaneous and unscripted few minutes of pure joy. How was the romance with Kermit going?

"You journalists know that there are public and private stances," said Miss Piggy reproachfully. "Kermit cannot speak of me too much in a close way because many, many women will be hurt."

"Look," protested Kermit in that familiar nasally sing-song voice, "just trust the frog, okay? I'm telling you we will be spending Christmas separately."

The eternally put-upon Kermit was perfect for the role of the downtrodden clerk, Bob Cratchit. But was Miss Piggy not far too glamorous to play his wife?

"I put a tremendous amount of preparation each day into looking drab," she told me, coquettishly flicking back a blonde curl. What a line. What a dame.

Sadly, the intervening years never delivered the part Miss Piggy longed for. What she had in mind, she confided dreamily, was to be leading lady in a historical costume drama. Ivanhoe would be wonderful – but it had to be with Kermit.

"Good grief," said the little green frog, burying his head in his hands. The best interview ever.

The Undone Years

For 15 years I wrote a column for the Express & Star on family life. It was entitled Unclassified Rhodes and it brought more response from our readers than anything I had written before or since. It was more than a column. It was a weekly chat with people who had been through much the same sort of experiences as us at Chateau Rhodes. By far the biggest postbag came in response to this piece from February 1992, written just after my father died of cancer, aged 66:

Life goes on, as insistent and indifferent as ever. A few hours after my father died, the weather changed. The dank, week-long mist lifted off the meadows to reveal the new growth of another spring. The fresh, lush corn snaked away from the house in uncertain furrows like college scarfs laid side by side: green and brown and green. The wind stirred, rattling the newly pruned rose stems against our windows.

I collected his things from the hospital. Two green plastic bags, his old fawn dressing gown protruding from one, a green-and-black box of Kleenex from the other. I was glad to get away from the nurses. I know it cannot be easy for them, coping with death after death and the unpredictable, unrehearsed grief of so many strangers. But there was a professional mawkishness about them that unsettled me. Did we want to see the body? Would we like to hold his hand? And if we didn't, well, we could always come back later and see him in the chapel of rest and, oh, they had a lovely chapel of rest. I mean, tacky or what? My father is dead. Lord know where the spirit has gone but the one place from which it was most certainly absent was the corpse in room three.

The undertaker, too, was heavily into viewing bodies. They would bring him over from the hospital, she intoned reverentially. He would be in their chapel if we wanted to be with him for a little while. With him? We may be "with him" at his funeral service or in the Yorkshire Dales he loved or among those who valued him or in the buildings he created. We are certainly with him in the seats of his final folly in the long catalogue of Great Automobile Disasters. It is a beautiful, extravagant heap of Italian rubbish known as the Lancia Gamma Coupe. We are not "with him" in any sense, gazing into some waxy, rouged-up visage in a funeral director's chapel.

The registrar, into whose official secrecy I delivered the envelope from the hospital stamped "Confidential," was wonderful. She has logged hundreds of births and deaths, she ought to be punch-drunk immune on alternate hammerings of joy and despair five days a week. And yet it was as though this was the first untimely death she had registered. She is a state pen-pusher whose only job is to keep the statistics straight and yet she understood the loss, the undone years. She came far closer to what I was feeling than either the nurses or the undertaker.

That night, I lay awake for a while and wondered. He read so much, he knew so many things. Where does all the wisdom go? And what do we do with that bloody Lancia?

The wind stirred across the meadows. The damp, raw ends of the rose stems scudded and squeaked against the windows, like a child sobbing in the dark.

"They were a wall unto us. Both by night and day."

For a few years from 2007-2011, by an accident of geography, the Wiltshire town of Wootton Bassett became the focus of Britain's mourning as Union Jack-covered coffins passed through on the road from RAF Lyneham to Oxford. A simple mark of observance by a few local people grew into homecoming ceremonies attended by hundreds and sometimes thousands of people. In August 2011 the Queen granted the designation "Royal" to the town. It was many miles off the Express & Star circulation area but, as so often in our history, we recognised it as a great national event, of importance to our readers and I was sent to cover one homecoming, with a photographer. This, from July 2009 was the result and it's one of my favourite pieces:

It's a friendly little town. As we emerged from the church tea room into a July shower, an old chap shared his big golf umbrella with me and pointed to the tower of St Bartholomew and All Saints church in Wootton Bassett.

"When that bell starts ringing," he said in a rich Wiltshire accent. "There'll be a silence like you've never heard before." At 4.26pm bellringer Roger Haydock began tolling the tenor bell. It rang clear and solemn, one peal every four seconds. The effect was magical. For those of us who had been in London 12 years ago, it was the sort of silence we experienced when the coffin of Diana, Princess of Wales passed by. Yesterday was a long, long day in Wootton Bassett. Some of the thousands lining the main street had

been standing in the town for six hours or more. As with Diana's funeral, the early mood had been not entirely solemn. The pubs were open and packed; the church was empty. There was almost a carnival air, until that tenor bell reminded us what was coming. When the eight hearses arrived, silence fell like a thick blanket. The wind rattled the neatly lopped lime trees. A child cried. The funeral director moved to the front of the procession. He faced the leading vehicle, bowed his head and then theatrically raised and lowered his arms in greeting, like a great black bird folding its wings.

The weeping began. The shaven-headed lads who had come to bid their mates farewell had spent the morning sinking pints and bravely showing off their shirts bearing the felt-tip logo "Lost a friend – gained an angel". Now they faced the reality, in eight Union Jack-covered coffins, of pals who would never come home. Some threw flowers at the hearses. Some applauded, their uncertain, thin handclaps lapping into the distance like a vanishing stream.

It was a motley crowd with all sorts from Guards officers with gleaming Sam Browne belts to trippers in shorts and a bizarre collection of ex-servicemen bikers wearing medal, berets and leathers complete with Ozzy Osbourne logos. Soldiers, sailors and RAF personnel lined the route. Standard bearers were allocated their places early and when TV cameras muscled in, a tetchy town mayor, Steve Bucknell, sent the crews packing.

I found no-one in Wootton Bassett with a bad word for today's soldiers, and no-one with a good word for the Afghanistan adventure.

"We were bluffed into that war," seethed on old chap in the churchyard. "Bluffed into doing the Yanks' work for them."

Inside the church, two plaques recall the twenty-five men of the town killed in the Second World War and the forty-six lost in the

First. Behind a posy in the church you can find a reminder, from the book of Samuel, of the simple, age-old relationship between civvies and soldiers: "The men were very good unto us, And we were not hurt. They were a wall unto us, Both by night and day."

Eight good men, part of that big camouflage-clad wall that protects this nation, passed before us. And when they had gone from our sight, a group of their loved ones embraced each other in the main street of Wootton Bassett, moving like one big, suffering creature as they howled in pain and grief.

The EU Referendum – one vote, two columns

I'm not going to dwell on politics or politicians. Out in the provinces we meet the giants of Whitehall rarely and probably don't spend enough time with them to form a balanced opinion. It might be unfair, for example, for me to claim on the strength of occasional encounters that Tony Blair was shifty, John Major was dull, Gordon Brown was weird, Paddy Ashdown was a star and John Smith, usually described as the best leader Labour never had, was a bad-tempered man who shouted at me on our first meeting and grabbed my tape-recorder and tried to switch it off on our second. My view, for what it's worth, is that Smith would have made a disastrous leader and was massively outclassed by Tony Blair, for all his faults. Let us leave the politicians for another time.

Anyway, the people who change the world and make it a better or worse place tend not to be political animals or, for that matter, celebrities but ordinary people. I wrote during the early days of the 2020 pandemic that the next Honours List from Buckingham Palace should be made up of doctors, nurses, supermarket staff, delivery drivers and all the others who kept us alive and ensured the system ticked over until times got better. In fact, the greatest tribute to the perfect Honours List would be for it to be read by folk who would remark: "You know, I've never heard of any of these."

Politically, in 100 years the Express & Star shifted from its founding principle of anti-monarchist republicanism to mainstream liberalism and finally to that vague concept known as one-nation Toryism. From the earliest days of the Common Market, the E&S took the view that the "minor loss of sovereignty" pledged by Edward Heath and others, was actually a major change in the way Britain was governed. The newspaper became Eurosceptic long before the term was fashionable. As the 2016 EU Referendum approached, the newspaper prepared its coverage for the great night. No-one seriously expected Britain would vote to leave the European Union but our most pressing problem was deadlines. There simply wouldn't be time to wait for the result (especially if there was a recount) and then write an assessment. The technology may have changed dramatically since the Charles & Di royal wedding of 1981 but the eagerness of editors to have words set in type and safely on a page continues.

So I was given the task of writing two personal pieces, one assuming the vote went Remain the other in case it was Leave. Clearly, one would have to be thrown away, but what else could we do? Here are the intros of those two pieces as a self-confessed Brexiter applauded a vote to quit the EU and lamented a vote to remain. First, if Remain won:

So farewell, the dream. It would have been wonderful to stop being Little Europeans and become Great Britons again. But the people have spoken. They have voted for what they perceive as the safe, the wise option. And so here we are, a timid island clinging to the teat of Mother Brussels, probably for centuries to come. Britain this morning is like the spouse who has threatened to walk out on their abusive partner. We have had the rows, we have dragged our luggage into the hall. Yet instead of going, we are sitting on our suitcases, begging for a second chance. To make it worse, all those neighbours who scoffed and sneered and said we'd never have the balls to walk out are cackling in the street outside. When it came to the vote, Great Britain wasn't so great after all, n'est ce pas?

And this if, by some miracle, the vote went for Brexit:

God, this feels good. The people have spoken. The people are packing their bags and leaving a place where we never felt fully at home. After 40-odd years of dithering, we can arise and be a nation. There are few events in history that raise the spirits in such a way. The fall of the Berlin Wall springs to mind, or the Blairs' triumphant entry into Downing Street in 1997 when even some Tories rejoiced to see a new broom in Number Ten. This feeling is a combination of knowing that an idea has reached its time, and possessing the power to make it happen. Rejoice, for we still live in a working democracy. We are righting a wrong that has haunted this nation for more than four decades.

I was surprised, but not as surprised at the result as some other pundits. Weeks before, when David Cameron announced the Referendum, the E&S held an online poll for its readers: Stay or Remain? Newspaper polls are hardly a scientific study and in their early hours can be skewed by a small number of votes. I logged in to our poll, just to get some steer on public opinion on our patch. The Leave vote was massively ahead with 86 per cent of votes. Clearly, I thought, this was an anomaly. Better give it 24 hours and see how the voting settles down. I checked again the next day. This time the Leave vote was 92 per cent.

The Black Country is hardly a barometer for the entire UK. But right from the early days of the campaign, if you looked hard enough, it was clear that out there in the provinces, ignored or overlooked by the mainstream national media, were many hundreds of thousands of people – some of whom never voted in other elections – who for all sorts of reasons wanted to leave the EU. And, to the astonishment of the BBC, ITV and most of Fleet Street, that's what happened.

Maybe the lesson will be learned. If you want to know which way the wind is blowing, by all means talk to a Professor of Advanced Wind-Blowing at the University of Gusts. So long as you also have a five-minute chat with an electrician from Walsall.

A reader writes...

For the past 35 years I have had columns of various sorts at the Express & Star. The latest which has been running for 20 years, is a daily reflection on politics, current affairs, cinema, TV, the theatre and anything else that looks intriguing or amusing. The great joy is the response it brings from readers, sometimes making profound and lengthy political points and sometimes just sending in a silly gag or a one-liner that has caught their eye. Thus:

I told my girlfriend I had a job in a bowling alley. She said 'Tenpin?' I said, 'No, permanent.'

I have taken to drinking brake fluid. I can stop any time.

Due to an unfortunate spacing error while booking our holiday this year, I am now looking forward to a week on the Norfolk B roads.

At a carol concert, I swear I heard: "Bring me pine logs, Hitler."

Regarding the news of horse meat found in "beef," I bought some burgers at the weekend … and they're off!

I won an award for my punctuation. They gave me a posh trophy.

A reader asks: "If I sponsor a South African antelope at my local zoo, could I ask for it to be called Vlad the Impala?"

More curious married names. A reader informs me that her friend Gail married Mr Whale.

Another recalls that his father's aunt was born Alice Ann Taylor Monks, and married a man called Taylor to become Alice Ann Taylor Taylor.

And yet another writes: "My Aunt Valerie married a Mr Gallery."

On the process of getting old, a reader offers this prayer: "Grant me the senility to forget the people I never liked, the good fortune to remember the ones I do, and the eyesight to tell the difference."

Many thanks to the reader who sent me the instructions for a kitchen timer, made in China, which includes the useful advice:

"Peg out the new battery plus or minus very put into, and press back the nome position the battery door."

I asked for examples of English signs in foreign places. A reader recalls this, seen in a hotel bedroom in Budapest: "Guests are invited to take advantage of the chambermaid."

Edukashun corner. A reader reports the latest baked-beans offer at his local supermarket: two tins for £1 or a pack of four tins for £2.50.

I wrote recently about Arthur Wynne who invented the cross-word puzzle 100 years ago. My thanks to all of you who have written to let me know his plot in the cemetery is 4 across and 6 down.

A reader tells me he missed the Doctor Who 50th anniversary special at the weekend but is planning to catch it in 1957.

The Black Country – an appreciation

I never regretted staying with the Express & Star. Over the years I had a couple of approaches from the BBC, a couple of interviews for Fleet Street and a contract as a TV producer-presenter signed, sealed and ready to be delivered. But each time, I thought again and decided to stay. I was born in Yorkshire, raised in Lancashire, Herefordshire, Oxfordshire and Warwickshire. I am essentially a provincial, and comfortably so.

"We liked you," a local-radio boss told me after interviewing me for a broadcast job and deciding not to make an offer. "The problem was, you created the impression that you wanted this job at the least possible inconvenience to yourself." Precisely. And why not?

If, as Dr Johnson suggested, "the noblest prospect which a Scotchman ever sees is the high road that leads him to England," then the noblest prospect for me is that moment on the Euston to Coventry line when the Great Wen vanishes and green fields appear. I have no desire to live in the capital, nor to commute vast distances to get there. I never felt cramped in Wolverhampton nor yearned for any bigger canvas that that afforded me by the unlovely slab of post-industrial England we call the Black Country. The Express & Star sent me to places I could only have dreamed of, to meet people at the top of politics, showbiz and real life.

If the newspaper founded by Andrew Carnegie had one guiding motto which set it apart from other newspapers it was "Words written well, sell." It is the job of every writer on the paper to produce the best copy they can, to make the reader think: "That was a damn good read tonight. I'll buy it again tomorrow."

And the people! The people are terrific. There is a wonderful dry, self-effacing humour that goes with the Black Country (never to be confused with Birmingham, thanks). You'll hear it not only in the jokes and anecdotes of Frank Skinner and Sir Lenny Henry but in every man and woman from a region whose proudest boast is "Ar bay from bloody Brum." In war and peace they are solid, phlegmatic, reliable, unruffled.

A few years ago BBC Radio 4 decided to do a couple of programmes on Black Country humour and got in touch with me to pick my brains. I steered them towards some of the lesser-known Black Country comedians and, when it was all done, the producer said he'd like me to sign off the programmes by telling my favourite Black Country joke. I declined for two reasons. Firstly, my home town is Leamington

Spa and I'm never going to sound like a Black Country man – pronounced mon. Secondly, my favourite yarn is not a joke but a true story involving an old friend called John who is an inventor. He spent some time in local factories, checking that his inventions were being properly used. He arrived at one little factory in Dudley just after one of the workers, in a dreadful accident with a machine, had sliced off his thumb. He was sitting, pale as frost, in shock with his thumb in a jam jar of ice beside him. His wounded hand was covered with a big, bloody bandage.

"How are yer feeling, mate?" inquired a colleague. The wounded man did not answer but smiled grimly and extended his arm and then turned his wrist through 90 degrees. And that's how you do a thumbs-down gesture when you haven't got a thumb. Even at a moment like that the Black Countryman makes a joke.

Let me finish with a tale from Dunkirk, 1940 when the Black Country lads of the Sixth Battalion the South Staffordshire Regiment were on the dunes, dodging Stuka bombs and waiting to be evacuated back to England. None of these Territorials would claim that they were the bravest or the most dashing of soldiers sent over to France. They knew they had been well and truly defeated by the advancing Germans.

Yet none of the survivors I interviewed in the spring of 2010, seventy years after Dunkirk, recalled any panic or pushing on the beaches.

On the contrary, these Territorials were so well led and bound together by such a strong community spirit and by the Black Country sense of humour, that something extraordinary began to happen. Sergeant-majors kept them busy with PE and drill. Someone found a couple of dispatch-rider bikes and organised races along the sands. The battalion buzzed with confidence and a sense of purpose; there was no question of defeat. Stragglers from other regiments, unsure what to do next, drifted across and attached themselves to the unit. Which is why this battalion has the distinction, which may be unique in the history of the British Expeditionary Force, of bringing more soldiers out of France than it took in.

Back then, in the bleakest days of the war, it was impossible to know how we would win. But with men like that, how could we possibly lose?

That spirit endures today in the Black Country. A great place. Great people. And it has been a great experience working among them and writing for them, and about them. Bloody adjectives and all.

About The Author

For more than a quarter-century Peter Rhodes was chief feature writer with Britain's biggest regional evening newspaper, the Express & Star at Wolverhampton. It was a career in the provincial press that many Fleet Street journalists would have envied, taking Rhodes around the world from the North Pole to the Falklands, from Hong Kong and Vietnam to South Africa by way of the first Gulf War, the Siege of Sarajevo, the Sri Lankan civil war and the first Palestinian intifada. He mixed with princes and paupers, great actors and leading politicians and military heroes. He chronicled some of the greatest events of the 21st century, sharing his award-winning dispatches with up to a million readers, chiefly in the old industrialised region of the West Midlands known as the Black Country. In Bloody Adjectives he looks back on a lifetime in journalism.